CREATIVE
GAMES
IN GROUPWORK

CREATIVE
GAMES
IN GROUPWORK

Robin Dynes

WINSLOW

Telford Road • Bicester
Oxon OX6 0TS • UK

First published in 1990 by
Winslow Press Ltd, Telford Road, Bicester, Oxon OX6 0TS, UK
www.winslow-press.co.uk
Reprinted 1991, 1992, 1993, 1994, 1995, 1996, 1997, 1998, 1999, 2000

Phototypeset by Gecko Limited, Bicester, Oxon

002-0499/Printed in the United Kingdom/1010

British Library Cataloguing in Publication Data
Dynes, Robin
    Creative games in groupwork
    1. Man. Psychosocial development. Teaching aids. Games.
    Collections
    1. Title
    302

ISBN 0 86388 078 9

CONTENTS

ROBIN DYNES has worked in an acute psychiatric hospital, been in the probation service and supervised youth groups. He is currently employed in the occupational therapy department of a psychiatric day hospital where he runs a variety of groups which include social and creative activities.

Robin is also the author of *Creative Writing in Groupwork*, an activity manual specifically designed to encourage people to express themselves through writing.

EDITOR'S NOTE
For the sake of clarity alone, in this text 'he' has been used to refer to the individual player.

FOREWORD

It gives me pleasure to be asked to write the foreword to Robin Dynes' book *Creative Games in Groupwork*. In particular I am pleased because it is a book with no pretensions. It sets out to describe clearly and lucidly the practical 'know-how' of a large number of games which are suitable for people of all ages and a wide range of capabilities.

We all play games for a variety of reasons and it is part of our human development that we can all remember games from our childhood — favourite games that we repeated and those games we dreaded — but we all have game memories. Games are an important part of play activity, so essential to human development in all cultures. In my own work as a dramatherapist I have been intrigued to discover how some games appear in a variety of cultures with local elaborations. For example, 'What's the Time Mr Wolf?' became 'Where are you Mr Tiger?' in Malaysia.

Games are fun — they enable us to work together and co-operate as well as compete in a non-destructive way; games keep us alert and develop body and mind in a non-pressurised way. Games, because they have rules, help us to contain our energy and direct it in a positive way. Games are meant to be enjoyed, which provides a marvellous antidote to the idea that work is not to be enjoyed!

This book gives a short clear introduction as to why games are important and the benefit to be derived from them. It then describes a large number of games — some familiar, some less well known — in a clear descriptive format. These are all games that can be adapted to our work-setting with a range of clients. The author has given us a wealth of information in one compact resource and it is one that we can continue to return to, especially when we feel like playing a game too!

Dr Sue Jennings
Director, The Institute of Dramatherapy
London 1990

ACKNOWLEDGEMENTS

Few of the games and ideas in this book are original. They have been passed down from generation to generation, remembered from childhood and school, passed on by colleagues, friends and the many participants in hundreds of groups. That is how it is with games.

I am grateful to Barbara Kilburn, Head Occupational Therapist at St Ann's Hospital, Poole, and Adele Watson, formerly Senior Occupational Therapist at St Ann's Hospital, Poole, and now living in Portugal, both of whom encouraged me to write this book.

The text owes much to my wife, Jean, who cast her professional eye over the manuscript to make sure it was readable.

PREFACE

WHY HAS THIS BOOK BEEN WRITTEN?

Picture the scene. Everyone is crowded around desks, busy planning groups, discussing, desperately searching for something new. I say: "What we need are more books with games and ideas!" There is an immediate silence. Suddenly a loud voice breaks the hush: "*You're* a writer! Why don't *you* write one?"

That search for something fresh to do, something different to please wide-ranging tastes in games, is never-ending for the group leader or teacher. Balance and variety is required in a programme in order to motivate different people: silly games, noisy games, quiet games, active and inactive games are necessary to suit all situations. At the same time these games must be capable of being adapted to achieve positive aims and support other activities in a social programme or one concerned with development or treatment.

The aim of this book is to help fill that need, by providing material which can be developed, adapted and used as a tool.

WHAT IS IN IT?

Scores of ideas for games, including comments regarding approach, attitudes and aims. Section 1 provides useful notes for those new to games and information on how to use the book. Sections 2–10 contain the games themselves.

If you do not agree with any of the rules, can think of better variations or do not like the approach suggested, do it your way. If the book stimulates ideas and enthusiasm it will have served its purpose.

WHO IS IT FOR?

People organising activities programmes. These include occupational therapists, nurses, teachers, social workers, students and guide, scout and church leaders. Most of the games can be adapted and used successfully with groups of all ages.

Robin Dynes

A GUIDE TO CREATIVE GAMES IN GROUPWORK

WHY GAMES?

Because they are a natural, playful means of learning and expression enjoyed from childhood. They provide experience in a sheltered environment, promote good atmosphere, relieve tension, break down social barriers, build morale and confidence and lessen fear more easily than does any other method. They provide a use for knowledge and skill and give incentive for acquiring these attributes. Games stimulate the imagination, make people resourceful and help develop social ability and co-operation. They can be used to reinforce other activities such as social skills and to stimulate expression. From them we can learn how to deal with day-to-day problems. Our general knowledge is improved when games are linked to subjects such as history, art and music.

Groups can use games for many different purposes and derive a variety of benefits from them. The following are some of the purposes for which the games in this book have been used:

- ▶ initiating conversation
- ▶ developing conversation
- ▶ increasing awareness
- ▶ building trust
- ▶ helping poor memory
- ▶ aiding clarity of speech
- ▶ motivating interest
- ▶ breaking down social isolation
- ▶ stimulating imagination and creativity
- ▶ improving concentration
- ▶ building self-confidence
- ▶ helping perception and observation
- ▶ increasing bodily skills
- ▶ making physical contact
- ▶ improving eye contact

- ▶ social development
- ▶ aiding interaction within groups
- ▶ increasing self-esteem
- ▶ improving thinking ability
- ▶ learning to accept responsibility
- ▶ making decisions
- ▶ learning to work with others
- ▶ promoting the ability to explore a situation
- ▶ promoting sensitivity
- ▶ improving judgement
- ▶ relaxation
- ▶ relieving anxiety
- ▶ developing ideas
- ▶ fun and enjoyment

The above list is no more than an indication of how the games may be used. Many other benefits and purposes can be derived.

HOW THE GAMES ARE PRESENTED

MATERIALS

Materials needed for each game are listed. These are given in a basic form and can be made more elaborate if this is thought necessary. Pencil-and-paper games can often be played orally, but pencils and paper have been recommended when more thought is required.

PREPARATION

Preparation for the games is clearly explained. This can take time but, where it is necessary, most of the games can be used again and again, making the effort well worth while.

ACTION

Action required for playing the games is given in a manner which allows group members as much freedom for self-rule as possible. The organiser may encourage teams and members to make their own decisions, thereby occupying them and giving them responsibility. Sitting people in a circle, as suggested in many of the games, is a good way of giving everyone the same status and encourages eye contact. The leader, however, should maintain overall control and be the final judge in any disputes.

Some methods of scoring are suggested to encourage competitiveness, but this is not compulsory. Indeed individuals can get very discouraged when thrown into competition. A way of avoiding this, yet still maintaining a competitive spirit, is to form teams. This introduces a more healthy form of competition by encouraging everyone to do their best for the team. Care should be taken when selecting players to ensure that teams are evenly matched and have an equal chance of winning.

VARIATIONS

Variations for the games are provided which can be enlarged upon. Often suggestions are given to show how the game can be adapted for teams and vice-versa.

4

COMMENTS

Comments are intended as useful hints and suggestions about the use of the game.

For ease of reference and selection the games have been divided into nine sections. Some of the games lend themselves to easy adaptation for use under several section headings. Feel free to use them in this manner. The games are not in any order of difficulty. While some are obviously harder than others, a great deal will depend upon the range of abilities to be found within the group. By altering the presentation, most of the games can be made easier or more difficult to suit. Where a game, or a particular version of it, has been found to be especially difficult, this is stated.

USING THE BOOK

Everyone develops their own style and method for making their group successful. What works for one person with a particular group will not necessarily work for another running a different group. Here are some points to bear in mind when choosing games and to help make your group successful.

1 Be enthusiastic.

2 Plan the session.

3 Give thought to the sequence of games; make sure there is variety — follow an inactive game with something active.

4 Take into account the needs of group members and their ability to interact with each other.

5 Be aware of the players' ability to concentrate. Adapt games so that they are challenging but do not run too long — games can be lengthened or shortened.

6 Choose games suitable to the size of the group and the space available for the activity.

7 Adapt the games to make them interesting to suit ages, interests, abilities and so on.

8 Make sure that you are familiar with the game and can explain it easily.

9 Do not keep people waiting.

10 Introduce the game in a manner which sets the tone and explains why it is being played.

11 Do any preparation before starting the game. Have all the

materials to hand. There should be no long gaps while you run out to photocopy something or decide what to do next.

12 Be prepared to act as a role-model and take part in the game.

13 Do not be a know-all!

14 Repeat and clarify instructions for those who did not hear or understand.

15 Give plenty of praise and encouragement.

16 Assist individuals who are having difficulty to participate.

17 Sense the changing moods of the group while playing and vary the programme accordingly, perhaps by changing the tempo, including an extra game or staying with something they find interesting and leaving something else out.

18 Respect the players' right not to share feelings, emotions and private information about themselves.

19 Have a sense of humour.

20 At the end of the game or session, summarise what has been achieved and discuss as necessary. If the game is purely for enjoyment this can be done by showing interest in whether or not people enjoyed it.

21 Keep a record of each session and how each game went. This can be used to plan future sessions.

WORKING THE MAGIC

Over and above everything else an enthusiastic approach is needed. This becomes infectious. Also, a sense of fun and enjoyment are essential in order to instigate the necessary feeling so that people can learn while playing. This is the essence of games playing. The more mental and physical effort applied, the more enthusiasm will be generated within the players. If you, as leader, enjoy the games, the more chances there are that the magic will work for everyone else.

GETTING TO KNOW YOU

A selection of introduction and mixing exercises

SPIN THE PLATE

MATERIALS

A plate or other object which will spin easily.

PREPARATION

A list of forfeits. Examples are:

1 Recite the alphabet.
2 Walk to a door and back.
3 Read or recite a poem.
4 Approach another group member and make a complimentary remark.
5 Walk around the room balancing a book on your head.
6 Do five press-ups.
7 Give a one-minute nonsense talk.
8 Touch your toes ten times.
9 Make a funny, sad or happy face.
10 Tell a funny story.

ACTION

Everyone sits in a circle. Ask all players to state their names and then invite one to stand in the centre of the circle. This person spins the plate on its edge and, while it is rotating, calls out the name of another participant, who leaps up and grabs the plate before it stops spinning. This person then spins the plate again and calls out another name. And so the game proceeds. If a player fails to catch the plate and it falls flat this person must pay a forfeit, then taking a turn to spin the plate and call out another name.

VARIATIONS

The game can be simplified by leaving out the forfeits or added to by having the players think up a forfeit every time someone fails to catch the plate.

COMMENT

This game is fun and helps the participants learn each other's names. It exercises concentration and memory as well as providing physical movement. The forfeits should be compiled to suit the group as regards age, abilities and so on.

NAME GAME

MATERIALS

None.

PREPARATION

None.

ACTION

Ask the group to sit in a circle. Request that a volunteer states his name and something about himself that he doesn't mind sharing with the group. The player on his right then repeats what the first player has said, states his own name and makes a statement about himself. The person on his right now repeats what participants one and two have said, says his own name and shares his personal detail with the group. This procedure continues round the circle.

VARIATIONS

1   The game can be kept simple by merely having everyone repeat the names in this manner.
2   Players may complete a supplied statement. An example would be: 'I went to market and bought . . .'. In this instance the first player might say: 'I went to market and bought a shirt.' The second player repeats this and adds an item of his own. The third player repeats both statements and adds a further article. And so the game continues round the circle. Other useful beginnings could be:
   a)   I'm going on holiday so I packed . . .
   b)   I went shopping for Christmas and bought . . .
   c)   I went to a party and took . . .
   Many other statements can be invented to suit any type of group.

COMMENT

An excellent memory game which is fun to play. If players have difficulty remembering, clues can be given by other members of the group to act as prompts. After completing the circle a discussion on how members of the group remember things can be useful.

STATIONS

MATERIALS

None.

PREPARATION

None.

ACTION

Seat everyone in a circle. Have each player call out his name and then ask one member of the group to go into the centre of the circle. Remove this player's chair from the circle. The person in the centre now calls out the names of two participants who must race across the circle to exchange positions. The player in the centre attempts to get into one of the vacant seats while the exchange of positions is taking place. If he succeeds, the person remaining unseated stays in the centre and calls out two more names. The player in the centre remains there until he is successful in taking another participant's seat.

COMMENT

If the players are elderly or the game becomes too rough it may be necessary to make a rule that everyone walks when changing places. In which case anyone who runs can be penalised by having to go in the centre.

AUTOBIOGRAPHIES

MATERIALS

None.

PREPARATION

None.

ACTION

Have each player choose a partner. Allow two or three minutes for each person to introduce himself to his companion. Encourage participants to help each other by asking questions such as 'Where were you born?', 'Have you any hobbies?'. When the time is up, have each set of partners join up with another, forming groups of four people. Each person must now introduce their partner to the new members of the group stating all the things known from the former conversation. Allow five minutes or so for this and then have each set of partners move on to form a new group of four, all of whom go through the same procedure again. This continues until each player has had an opportunity to meet everyone else.

VARIATION

A simpler version of this activity would be to have each player find a partner, introduce himself and then, having found out about his new acquaintance, introduce that person to the whole group. Two or three minutes should be sufficient time for the partners to find out about each other before forming a circle for the introductions to the group.

COMMENT

A good mixing activity which helps with self-awareness, trust and social development.

SELF-INTRODUCTION

MATERIALS

None.

PREPARATION

None.

ACTION

Have everyone sit in a circle. Tell the group that you want each player to introduce himself by name and to give a short talk about himself, saying everything that he would like the others to know about him. Make a rule that no one must talk for longer than either one or two minutes. Give a few seconds for thought and ask a volunteer to begin, or give an example by starting the ball rolling yourself.

VARIATIONS

1   Simplify the above by asking each player to state his name and three things about himself. These could be: a hobby, place of birth, a favourite colour and so on.

2   Have each player state his name and an item of good news he has had during the past week. He might say that he has received a letter from a friend, been on an outing or been given a present.

3   Ask each player to say his name and relate a funny or amusing incident which has happened to him in the past.

COMMENT

The number of variations on the above are numerous and the game can be adapted to suit any purpose. Some more suggestions:

a)   relate an earliest memory;

b)   state what you would like to happen in the near or distant future;

c)   share your happiest moment or the happiest time in your life;

d)   air your moment of greatest embarrassment;

e)   tell about an incident or happening which has changed the course of your life.

WHICH FLOWER?

MATERIALS

Pens, card, glue, magazines, seed adverts, scissors.

PREPARATION

Cut pictures of plants and flowers out of seed catalogues, gardening magazines and so on. Glue them to card and number each one. Make a list of the plant names, making sure that the numbers on the list correspond with the numbers on the cards.

ACTION

Place the pictures on various surfaces around the room. Tell the group how many there are and ask them to circulate and write down the names of each plant or flower. Encourage discussion within the group regarding varieties and so on. The purpose is to get people mixing and talking to each other. Allow a set time, depending on the number of pictures, then sit everyone in a circle and, holding up each picture, have players call out the answers. Either go round the group one by one or have them call out collectively.

VARIATIONS

This is a game with a vast range of variations. Instead of flowers use cars — old or modern — birds, animals, cities, famous buildings, film stars, famous personalities, machines — both ancient and modern — fish, famous ships, guns, pop groups, royalty and so on. The list is endless.

COMMENT

It takes some initial effort to collect and prepare the pictures for this type of quiz but, once completed, they can be used time and time again. Also, once a number of them have been prepared, the same quiz need never be used with the same group twice.

JOURNALIST

MATERIALS

Pencils and paper.

PREPARATION

None.

ACTION

Stage I   Divide the players into two groups and ask them to form two rows facing each other. If there are an equal number of men to women make sure each player has a partner of the opposite sex. Explain that you want the partners to make conversation, finding out as much as possible about each other in the three or four minutes allowed. Encourage players to ask each other questions and to volunteer information if partners become stuck.

Stage II   When the time limit has arrived send one group into another room. Give everyone a pencil and a piece of paper. Ask them to pretend to be a journalist and write a short piece about their partner for the local paper. This will comprise a description and as much information derived from the previous conversation as possible.

Stage III   Bring the two groups back together again and sit in a circle. Have everyone read out in turn what they have written and see how observant they have been. Give the person being written about an opportunity to correct any errors of memory and so on.

COMMENT

It is important to give the players only enough instruction to complete one stage of this game at a time. The game is a good observation and memory exercise. If players are encouraged to make positive comments on appearance and character it aids in building self-confidence and self-esteem.

WORD HUNT

MATERIALS

Pencil, paper, card, scissors.

PREPARATION

Make a list of six-letter words, the same number as there are players in the group. Give each word a number. Cut card into square pieces and write the letters of each word on the pieces — one letter to each card. Make sure you number the letter cards to correspond to your word list. Mix all the letters up and place them around the room. Write out slips of paper which say: 'Your word has six letters, each of which is numbered . . .' Insert one of the word numbers in the blank space.

ACTION

Give each player a slip of paper and ask him to find the letters. The first player to do this and make a word out of them is the winner.

VARIATIONS

1   Instead of letters on the cards write words which can be made into famous quotations or proverbs.
2   Have the letters make titles of books, authors, film stars, song titles, politicians, names of animals, birds, flowers or any other subject.

COMMENT

A game which can be made difficult by using longer words or easier by using shorter words. When it is used to aid mixing, encourage players to help each other and exchange ideas.

WHAT DO YOU SEE?

MATERIALS

Pens, magazine pictures, card, glue, scissors, paper.

PREPARATION

Cut out pictures from magazines, each as large as possible and containing lots of different types of objects and scenery. Paste these onto card or large sheets of paper. Label each picture with a letter of the alphabet, leaving out the more difficult letters like X, Y and Z.

ACTION

Place the pictures around the room or hang the sheets of paper around the walls. Instruct the players to look at the pictures and note down as many items as possible in each picture beginning with the letter written on it. Give a time limit. When this is up, sit everyone down and ask players to shout out what has been observed in each picture. The winner can be the player with the greatest number of objects listed or the most items no one else has noticed.

COMMENT

Encourage players to discuss the pictures as they mingle. This is a good observation game. When choosing the pictures bear in mind the ages and interests of the participants. Try to include the type of pictures which are most likely to stimulate them.

WHAT AM I?

MATERIALS

Pencils, paper, pins.

PREPARATION

Write the name of an animal on one side of a sheet of paper for each player. Make a list of the animals.

ACTION

Give each player a sheet of paper, a pencil and a pin. Instruct players not to let anyone else see the written name and to draw the animal on the other side of the sheet. Allow a few minutes and then have each player pin his animal to his chest. Now have everyone circulate with pencil and paper, writing down as many of the animals as they can guess. The person who has the most correct is the winner.

VARIATIONS

Instead of animals, use birds, fish, flowers, trees and so on.

COMMENT

This game can be made as easy or as difficult as you wish. Animals such as cows, sheep and dogs are easy. More obscure animals, like bison, walrus, weasel, otter, would make it difficult.

WHO AM I?

MATERIALS

Pen, labels and pins.

PREPARATION

Write the names of famous people on the labels.

ACTION

Pin a label, bearing the name of a famous person, on each player's back. Don't let him see the name. Request that people circulate and ask questions of other participants, the aim being to discover the name on the label attached to their own backs. This can be made more difficult by allowing only 'yes' or 'no' answers, or making a rule that each player can ask only one question of each person approached. Examples of questions a player might ask are: "Am I still alive?", "Am I an entertainer?". "Do I live in this country?", "Do I appear on television?".

VARIATIONS

1   Instead of 'famous people' labels, consider using animals, birds, objects, titles of books, films, cities, countries, flowers, food and so on. The list of subjects is endless.

2   Use the names of famous couples, splitting the names between two labels. This time players must find out who they are, then find their partners. You can also use things which go together for this variation. Examples might include salt and pepper, strawberries and cream, sugar and spice. Quotations can also be split into halves, as can authors and books, plays and playwrights, film stars and films, proverbs, pop stars and songs and so on.

COMMENT

A good mixing game which provides lots of fun. This activity is an excellent one for pairing players up in preparation for a follow-up game.

GUESS WHO?

MATERIALS

None.

PREPARATION

None.

ACTION

Sit the players in a circle and have them say their names. Allow time for everyone to have a good look at each other. Ask for a volunteer, who leaves the group and stands with his back to everyone. A player in the circle now describes another member of the group. The person with his back to the circle tries to guess who is being described. When he has done so, let someone else have a turn.

VARIATIONS

1   The player outside the circle asks questions to find the person the group have chosen.
2   Have the player describing the member of the group portray him in an opposite way. An example of this might be to say a thin person is fat.

COMMENT

Players can be described in a humorous or a positive manner, depending on whether you want to use this exercise for fun or positive reinforcement.

SNOWBALL TALK

MATERIALS

Pencils, paper, cassette and cassette-player or record and record-player.

PREPARATION

None.

ACTION

Stage I   Ask the players to choose a partner, shake hands and introduce themselves. When they have done so, explain that the object is to find out as much as possible about each other in one minute. When the minute is up, start the music, at which time everyone must find a new partner. When the music stops they will have another minute to shake hands and to discover as much as possible about this new person. Tell them that the procedure will continue in this manner for about ten minutes or until there has been sufficient opportunity for everyone to meet.

Stage II   Sit everyone in a circle and give out pencils and paper. Ask each player to write down the names of everyone to whom he has spoken and what he can remember about each person. Allow a few minutes and then ask each player to read out what he has written. Points can be given to players who pick up the most information or discover things which no one else has managed to learn.

VARIATIONS

1   Have the initial partners form an inner and outer circle facing each other. When the music is playing the inner circle moves to the right and the outer to the left. When the music stops, each player talks to the person opposite.

2   The game can be made more simple by asking players to remember names only.

COMMENT

This activity allows people to practise meeting and touching in a manner close to normal everyday living. The exercise can, of course, be done without music. However, music does provide an air of relaxation and adds to the game, especially when performed as fun. The game is also a good memory exercise.

I IMAGINE...

MATERIALS

None.

PREPARATION

None.

ACTION

Seat the group in a circle. One player turns to the neighbour on his left and, making an assumption, says: "I imagine that you are a butcher." The neighbour corrects the statement if it is wrong and explains something about himself. The player making the guess can also say what it was about his neighbour that made him think as he did. The neighbour now turns to the person on his left and makes another assumption beginning: "I imagine . . ." This continues round the circle.

VARIATIONS

1 The type of assumptions can be altered. Here are two examples:
   a) I see that you . . .
   b) Do you really believe that . . .?
2 Make a rule that each assumption must be wildly exaggerated or funny.

COMMENT

A game which is fun and prompts people to share information and allows them to learn something of how they appear to others.

ADVERTS

MATERIALS

Pencils, paper, card, adverts, scissors, glue.

PREPARATION

Cut out about twenty advertisements of well-known products from magazines or other sources. Either blank out or cut off the product names and paste the pictures to card. Number the advertisements. Make a list of the numbers and write down the product names. Ensure that the numbers on the advertisements and the product list correspond.

ACTION

Lay the advertisements on surfaces around the room. Make sure that they are not in sequence — you want the players to have to search for the numbers they need. Give the participants pencils and paper and ask them to list what they think are the product names. Encourage discussion and exchange of ideas. Allow about fifteen minutes to complete the list and then sit everyone down in a circle. Call out the numbers and let the players give the answers. The person with the most right is the winner.

VARIATIONS

1   To make this activity easier, write the product names on a blackboard or large sheet of paper, but list them out of sequence. Ask players to match the pictures to the product.
2   Give each player a prepared list of advertising slogans. Ask each person to look at the pictures and write down the product which goes with each slogan.
3   A selection of advertisements which are different but advertise the same product will provide some fun.

COMMENT

Preparation for this game is time-consuming but, once prepared, the advertisements can be filed and used frequently.

INTERVIEW

MATERIALS

None.

PREPARATION

None.

ACTION

Split the group into partners. Allow time for them to introduce themselves and to decide who is going to be A and who B. Explain that you want player A to interview B as a television interviewer might. A will want to find out about places where B has lived, his interests, his hobbies, where he has travelled, what job he does, his opinions on various topics, general philosophy on life, if he has children or grandchildren and so on. Allow about five minutes and then have B interview A.

VARIATIONS

1   If you want to make the exercise easier make out a short form indicating the type of questions players can ask. Let participants use this when doing the interview.

2   Give everyone pencil and paper and split the group into partners. Allow time for them to write down some information about each other. Next form a circle. Each player now takes turns at conducting his interview in front of the group, this time attempting to direct the interview to items of interest found out earlier about the interviewee. If you wish, this may be set up like a proper interview.

3   Form small groups of three or four people. Each group elects an interviewer who is given a little time to chat to the others. He then conducts his interviews in front of the other groups. End up by interviewing the group leaders yourself or have another group member do so.

4   Ask players to discover an item of interest about their partners. Examples might be: a recent holiday, a hobby, a particular job, the fact that they collect such items as stamps, enjoy a particular activity and so on. When interviewing, the purpose is to ask

questions in such a way as to draw out as much as possible about the particular topic in order to interest the group.

COMMENT

A helpful exercise for people who are hesitant about speaking in front of others. If you want to prepare a question list it is important to bear in mind the abilities of the players. Interviews can be conducted on a wide variety of subjects to create a great deal of fun. Here are a few suggestions:

a) The funniest thing that ever happened to me.
b) The weirdest thing that ever happened to me.
c) Regrets in my life.
d) Things I wish I'd done.
e) Things I want to do.

Suggested questions:

► Are you married?
► Have you any children?
► What do you do for a living?
► How did you come to be involved in that?
► Was it something you always wanted to do?
► Have you any hobbies or relaxation activities?
► How do you do that?
► Is that something everybody can do, or do you need particular skills?
► What tools do you need?
► How would someone new to the activity go about getting involved in it?
► Supposing you could have chosen a different country to live in — which country would it be?
► Is there anybody famous you admire?
► What are the qualities you admire in him?

And so on . . .

JIGSAW

MATERIALS

Pencils, paper, scissors, card, glue.

PREPARATION

Cut about twenty pictures out of magazines. These can be landscape scenes, groups of people, animals or objects of any sort. Cut the pictures into two or three pieces. Give each segment of picture a number and make a list of the numbers which make up each picture. Jumble the pieces and paste them onto large sheets of paper or card.

ACTION

Place the picture segments in different places around the room. When the players arrive ask them to study the cut-up pictures and list which numbers go together to make complete pictures. The winner can be the player with the most correct or the most completed number sets in a given time.

VARIATIONS

The game can be made easier by reducing the number of pictures or more difficult by cutting the pictures into four or five segments.

COMMENT

When selecting the pictures, bear in mind the interests of the players. Teenagers may appreciate and have more interest in pop groups and so on than in landscapes.

OBSERVATION QUIZ

MATERIALS

Pencils and paper.

PREPARATION

Make out a questionnaire. Here are some suggested questions:

1. What colour are your partner's eyes?
2. Are they wearing a ring or any other jewellery?
3. What type of footwear are they wearing?
4. What colour are their shoes?
5. What colour shirt/blouse are they wearing?
6. What colour is their hair?
7. Is their hair long or short?
8. Are they wearing glasses?
9. Are they taller or shorter than you?
10. What colour socks/stockings are they wearing?

ACTION

Have the players line up in two teams facing each other. Ask participants to introduce themselves to the person opposite and exchange information about their past, interests and so on. Allow about three minutes and then have the teams turn back to back. Better still, have one team go into another room. The important thing is that no one looks at their opposite number from this point on. Now give each player pencil, paper and the prepared list of questions (or call them out) allowing time between each question for the answer to be written down. When this is completed bring the teams back together as before, so all players can read out their answers and check their accuracy. Alternatively, form a circle and have the answers read out, giving the person being described a chance to correct any mistakes. The game can be played by dividing players into pairs, instead of teams.

VARIATIONS

1. Allow the players to view a prepared room for two minutes and then give them a questionnaire to answer.

2   Take everyone for a short walk and then find out how observant everyone has been.
3   Show a short video, some slides or even pass around some individual pictures and check for accuracy of observation.

COMMENT

If the partners are paired as male and female you can make out a separate questionnaire to suit. This type of quiz can also be adapted as a questionnaire on safety in the home. In this case, prepare a room, making sure that there are a number of health and safety risks. Note how many are observed and discuss the answers.

GUESS THE PHRASE

MATERIALS

Pencils, paper, card and objects to act as clues.

PREPARATION

Prepare a list of phrases and number them. Place objects which provide a clue to the phrase on numbered cards at various points around the room. Make sure that the card, object and phrase all relate correctly to the same number. Examples of objects and phrases are:

salt — salt of the earth

picture — pretty as a picture

pen and paper — put pen to paper

nail — hit the nail on the head

grass — snake in the grass

needle — sharp as a needle

feather — light as a feather

pot — keep the pot boiling

bonnet — bee in one's bonnet

water — fish out of water

rake — thin as a rake

brass — bold as brass

silk — soft as silk

brush — give the brush-off

glove — hand in glove

sugar — sweet as sugar

straw — the last straw

lead — heavy as lead

ACTION

Give the players pencils and paper. Ask them to use the objects as clues and guess the phrases you have listed. Encourage participants to mix, discussing each object and possible phrase. The player with the most correct wins.

VARIATIONS

1 Use drawings or pictures instead of objects.
2 Substitute similes or proverbs for phrases.
3 Flowers may also be used in place of phrases.

Examples:

butter and a cup — buttercup

picture of a fox and a glove — foxglove

corn and flour — cornflower

a sweet and a picture of William Shakespeare — sweet-william

picture of a wall and flour — wallflower

COMMENT

An activity to help people mix that is fun and exercises the imagination.

TASKS

MATERIALS

Pins, paper, pen and scissors.

PREPARATION

Write out a list of tasks for each player to perform. Also prepare some numbered labels: one for each participant. Examples of tasks:

1 Find out who number six is and ask him where he was born.
2 Introduce yourself to number five and find out four things he dislikes.
3 Approach number two, introduce yourself, and ask where he would like to go for a holiday.
4 Exchange views on pop music with number ten.
5 Introduce yourself to number eight and discuss favourite foods.

ACTION

Pin a number to each player's chest and give him the appropriate list of tasks to do. When everyone has completed his tasks, or an allowed time is up, sit everyone in a circle. Ask participants to share the information they have discovered about other players in the group.

VARIATIONS

1 The tasks may be made silly or humorous to keep this exercise on an amusing level.
2 Turn the tasks into questions, seeking opinions on various subjects, or enquiring how particular players would solve some problem situations.

COMMENT

An excellent mixing game which encourages people to carry out daily introduction and conversational tasks. The exercise can be shortened by not having players sharing information or by giving each person only two or three tasks to complete. Experience shows that five tasks is a good number to set.

GENTLY AS YOU GO

Quiet games, mostly using gentle movement

OCCUPATIONS

MATERIALS

Slips of paper and a bag.

PREPARATION

Write an occupation on each slip of paper and place them in a bag.

ACTION

This is a miming game. Seat the group so that the person doing the mime can be seen by everyone. Have a player come out and dip into the bag containing the pieces of paper. The participant then mimes a series of actions, imagining himself doing the job. The rest of the group try to guess what it is. Set a time limit, with points for players whose occupations are guessed.

VARIATIONS

1 Allow each member to think up the occupation he will mime.
2 Have the players mime a job they have done themselves.
3 Use as a team game. Each team has to guess an occupation mimed by a member of their own team.
4 Use other themes: hobbies, proverbs, titles of books, plants and so on.

COMMENT

A relatively easy game to play which encourages participation, especially when players mime an occupation they themselves have done. This also helps players get to know one another and share information. After each mime, use the exercise to encourage members to talk about their experience of the job, when applicable.

THE SPORTS GAME

MATERIALS

A blackboard and chalk or large sheets of paper and a magic marker. Also, some slips of paper and a small bag.

PREPARATION

Put pieces of paper containing the names of various sports into a bag.

ACTION

Invite a player to dip into the bag and pull out a piece of paper. He must then draw something on the blackboard to represent the sport. The other players try to guess what it is. Have a time limit and give points to the players whose sport is guessed before the time is up.

VARIATIONS

Many variations on this theme can be used. Here are a few:

nursery rhymes	proverbs
book titles	television programmes
songs	plays
films	quotations
countries	occupations

COMMENT

This also makes a good team game. Players from each team take turns at drawing a sport for their own team. A point is awarded if the team guesses before the time limit has expired. A popular game which stimulates quick thinking.

WHOSE HANDS?

MATERIALS

A bed sheet, pencils and paper.

PREPARATION

Hang the bed sheet up across a doorway so that no one can see into an adjacent room. Cut a slit in the sheet about waist high, large enough for a pair of hands to protrude.

ACTION

Divide the group into teams (ideally two teams, one of men and the other of women). The women go into the room behind the sheet and remove any rings from their fingers. One at a time they push their hands through the slit. Have them show the palms of their hands, to disguise any nail varnish. The men must identify each pair of hands by writing down the name of the person concerned. When all the women have shown their hands see how many of them have been correctly identified. The men then go into the adjoining room and follow the same procedure.

VARIATION

Have the players remove their shoes. This time raise the sheet about nine inches from floor level. The opposing team try to identify the owners of the exposed feet.

COMMENT

Before commencing the game make sure that group members are familiar with each other's names. To make remembering names easier, a list can be provided on a blackboard.

GONE FISHING

MATERIALS

String, two garden canes, two wire hooks, cotton reels or other suitable objects, and two wastepaper bins.

PREPARATION

Attach a piece of string to the end of the canes to make fishing rods. Tie the wire hooks to the end of the string. Also tie string loops on the cotton reels which can be hooked. Make two pools — this can be wastepaper bins or more elaborate creations — and place the cotton reels in them.

ACTION

Form the players into two teams. On the word 'go' a player from each team tries to hook a fish from his own pool. When he has done so, he returns to his team base and the next player has a turn. After a set time, stop the proceedings. The team with the most fish hooked is the winner.

VARIATION

Form the players into a large circle around a single pool. Give each person a fishing rod. On the given word, everyone starts fishing for a set length of time. The player with the most fish caught is the winner.

COMMENT

This is a good, light-hearted game which can be used between more strenuous or serious activities to lighten the session. It is always good fun.

PAPER-CLIP RACE

MATERIALS

Lots of large paper-clips.

PREPARATION

None.

ACTION

Line the players up into two or more teams. Give the leader of each team two paper-clips and the remainder of the team one each. On the word 'go' the leader joins up the two paper-clips and passes them on to the second player who joins his paper-clip to the original two. This continues down the line. When the last player has joined his clip to the others he walks quickly to the front with the chain of clips and hands them to the team leader. The leader then takes off one clip and passes the chain to the second player who removes another. This continues to the last player, who returns from the front to detach the last clip, holds it up in the air and yells, "Finished!" The first team to complete the task is the winner.

VARIATIONS

1   Have players select a partner. Give each pair the same number of paper-clips. One person makes the chain, then his partner undoes it.

2   Use beads and a piece of string instead of paper-clips. Team leaders are given a bead and a piece of string each. The other players have one bead. The object is to thread the beads onto the piece of string. The first team finished is the winner.

COMMENT

A game which is good fun and helps members to break down barriers and participate as part of a team. It is also useful as a session 'lightener'.

FASHION PARADE

MATERIALS

Sheets of newspaper or brightly coloured paper, sticky tape and scissors.

PREPARATION

None.

ACTION

Give each player two large sheets of paper, a roll of sticky tape and a pair of scissors. Tell participants that they have five minutes in which to design a hat. Instruct them to make it funny, artistic, or whatever they may choose. When the five minutes are up, have a fashion parade and let members vote for the best or most comic creation.

VARIATION

Have players choose a partner. Give each couple five or six sheets of paper. Explain that one person must design a garment for his partner. When this has been completed have a fashion parade with the designer introducing his design which is worn by his model. Let members vote for the garment which is the most fun.

COMMENT

To make the game easier and to encourage involvement of more reticent members, divide the players into small groups with two or three people designing a hat or garment for one person.

JUMBLED NEWSPAPERS

MATERIALS

Newspapers — preferably with large pages. Broadsheets are excellent, especially the larger Sunday editions. Make sure that all the papers used have the same number of pages.

PREPARATION

Taking each paper separately, jumble up the pages out of order and turn some pages upside down.

ACTION

Give each player a jumbled newspaper. On the word 'go' participants put the pages in the correct order. The first person finished is the winner.

VARIATIONS

1   Make the game more difficult by mixing the pages of two newspapers together for each player.
2   Mix the pages of different papers together and give each player some pages with instructions to find the pages of a specific newspaper. Each player has to find the other people who have the pages he requires for the task. The first person to complete the task is the winner.
3   Use as a team game with teams having to put together sets of papers which have been jumbled up.

COMMENT

A simple game which is a lot of fun.

RING ON A STRING

MATERIALS

A ball of string and a ring of some sort, which can be concealed in the palm of the hand.

PREPARATION

Thread the ring onto the string and join both ends of the string together so that it becomes a circle. Make sure that the string is long enough to be held in both hands by the group members when everyone is sat in a circle.

ACTION

When the group is sat in a circle and each player has both hands on the string, ask one person to stand in the middle. He then closes his eyes while those in the circle begin passing the ring from person to person on the string. After a moment, on a given word, the player in the middle opens his eyes. The player passing the ring along the string must try to conceal it in the palm of his hand. Also the ring must be kept continually on the move. The direction of passing can be changed at any time. The object is for the person in the centre to guess who has the ring. When he does, that player is the next to take a turn in the middle.

COMMENT

A low-key game which can be played by everyone and one which always delights.

BLIND MAN'S BUFF

MATERIALS

A blindfold.

PREPARATION

None.

ACTION

Have the group sit in a circle. Ask for a volunteer to sit in the centre. This person is blindfolded. All the other players now change places. When everyone has settled, the blindfolded person points in various directions and asks people to make noises. He can ask the person pointed at to make a specific noise: a cat miaow, to say "Ah!", boo, hiss or he can let the person choose his own sound. The object is to identify the person who is making the noise. Anyone who is recognised and named then takes a turn in the centre.

VARIATION

To make this game very easy, have the players speak or read a sentence from a book instead of making a noise.

COMMENT

It is a good idea to use one of the introduction exercises in *Section 2* of this book prior to this game, thus ensuring that all the players know each other by name and the sound of each other's voices. A good memory and concentration game.

MAKING A WILL

MATERIALS

Pencils and paper.

PREPARATION

None.

ACTION

Send one player out of the room. While he is out the group compile a list of effects — up to about twelve items. Number each one and make them as amusing as possible. Have them relate to hobbies and character as well as actual things. Examples:

love letters	rusty nails
old boots	a snuff box
a wig	a parrot
a sloppy grin	pickled onions
a wicked laugh	a silly walk
a wisdom tooth	a stuffed crocodile

When the list is complete and each item numbered, the exiled player is called back into the room. He is asked by an elected spokesman: "To whom or what do you leave item number one?" He replies: "A charity" or whatever else comes into his head, which might be: "To be buried at sea"; "To my Aunt Lily"; "My best friend" or "Margaret Thatcher."

The more ludicrous the answer the better. Then the item bequeathed is read out. When the list has been completed in this manner, another player is asked to leave the room.

COMMENT

Make sure that you brief the first player who goes out of the room. This enables him to think of how he will dispose of the items while he is waiting for the group to compile the list. Giving him a pencil and paper to write on is also helpful.

WHAT AM I LIKE?

MATERIALS

None.

PREPARATION

None.

ACTION

Ask one player to leave the room. Those who remain decide upon an object he will have to try to guess. Then the player is requested to return to the group. He approaches or points to a person of his choice and asks: "What am I like?". If the chosen object was a suitcase the player might answer: "Squarish, thick and flat." Another participant is then asked the same question: "What am I like?". He might answer: "Very useful." The questioning continues in the same manner until the player has guessed the object. Another person is then asked to leave the room.

VARIATIONS

Instead of "What am I like?", the questioner asks:
1   Why do you like me?
2   When do you like me?

COMMENT

A game which is fun and encourages quick thinking and helps to build confidence.

DEADPAN FACES

MATERIALS

None.

PREPARATION

None.

ACTION

Seat the group in a circle. Ask for a volunteer to act as leader. The leader then performs a silly act. This could be standing on one leg and scratching his head. Each person in the group must now — one at a time — do the same. When everyone else has had a go, the leader does something else silly such as tweaking his neighbour's ear, sniffing loudly, doing a mime or making a funny face. One at a time, the other players follow suit. This procedure continues until someone in the group breaks down and grins or laughs. He then becomes the leader. The object of the game is to keep a deadpan face.

VARIATION

One player holds up an empty picture frame — a cardboard one is ideal — through which he looks at the other players. Group members make funny faces, crack jokes, make funny remarks or do silly things to try to make him smile. If he lasts out for more than one minute he passes the picture frame on to the next player. If he laughs he must pay a forfeit.

COMMENT

For the variation it is a good idea to have the group shout out the forfeits before the game begins and write them up on a blackboard. If necessary those paying the forfeit can then choose their own. Also, do not allow forfeits to be of a nature to cause embarrassment. Usually keeping them to a simple action is adequate. Examples:

1   Relate something funny which has happened to you.
2   Repeat a tongue-twister. (Have one ready.)
3   Talk for one minute non-stop.

4   Juggle with three tennis balls. (Have the balls handy.)

5   Go up to one member of the group, look him in the eyes and say: "I admire you because . . ." (The other player completes the sentence.)

JUDGE THE MOOD

MATERIALS

None.

PREPARATION

None.

ACTION

Form the participants into a circle and ask one player to volunteer as judge. From the centre, he commands the others to express a mood or emotion. Examples:

anger	panic	joy
despair	boredom	pride
fear	anxiety	sadness

The judge awards points to the best actor interpreting each word. After a few words have been demonstrated, ask for another volunteer to be judge. Alternatively, have players call out an emotion in turn. Each player judges the word he calls out.

VARIATION

Write the moods or emotions on slips of paper, which are folded and placed in a bag. Have the players take turns at picking one out of the bag and enacting it. The other participants have to guess the emotion that is being expressed and award points.

COMMENT

Allow speech and/or gesture, or restrict merely to facial expression, depending on the degree of difficulty required for the aims of the group. This game is a good aid to expression, perception and ability to communicate feelings.

WHAT KIND OF HOLIDAY?

MATERIALS

None.

PREPARATION

None.

ACTION

Sit the players in a circle. Invite one person, who will be known as 'the questioner' to stand in the middle. The questioner names or approaches someone in the circle and asks: "What kind of holiday do you like?". This person must answer using words beginning with his own initials. His answer might be: "Climbing in Malta." The questioner then moves on to ask another player the same question. Any player who fails to think of an answer or repeats what he has said previously becomes the questioner. Limit the answers to an activity and a place name which can be a country, county, town or district.

VARIATIONS

Change the question to:
1   What kind of food do you like? (Curry from Madras.)
2   What kind of work would you like and where? (Carpentry in Manchester.)

COMMENT

A quick thinking game which combines inventive ability with a sense of fun.

COMMENT CARDS

MATERIALS

Cards, pencils and sticky tape or safety-pins.

PREPARATION

None.

ACTION

Tape or pin a card to each player's back. Instruct each person to circulate and write a word or phrase on the cards pinned to all other players' backs. The word or phrase should describe, or be a comment upon, the person on whose back the card is pinned. When each player has had his card written on the cards are unpinned and players read out their own personal cards. Have participants try to guess who has written what about them. Also, when appropriate, discuss the comments.

VARIATIONS

1   When it is necessary that participants have feedback for self-awareness, introduce the game in such a manner that a suitable attitude can be adopted by the players.

2   When positive reinforcement is required, ask the participants to write only positive comments.

3   Ask each person to write humorous, light-hearted or outrageous flattery about each other.

COMMENT

An exercise which can be put to a wide variety of uses, including making physical contact, increasing self-esteem, breaking down social isolation and increasing perception and observation.

RHUBARB

MATERIALS

None.

PREPARATION

None.

ACTION

Have the participants sit or stand in a circle with one person in the middle. The centre player approaches any other person and, looking him in the eyes, asks him personal questions. Examples:

"To what do you attribute your freckles?"

"What made you grow so tall?"

"What makes you smile?"

"What makes you blush?"

"To what do you attribute your tiredness?"

The player being questioned must answer each question with the word "Rhubarb". If he smiles or laughs he then becomes the questioner. If not, the questioner moves on and tries to make another player smile or grin.

VARIATIONS

An animal, a bird or a short phrase can be substituted for 'Rhubarb'. In fact, use any answer word which will sound comical, pretentious or daft. Examples might include snakes, potatoes, snails or gnomes.

COMMENT

A game which is fun and good for breaking down barriers and making people smile.

GUESS THE SOUND

MATERIALS

Pencils, paper, a selection of articles and a bag.

PREPARATION

Place some articles in a bag or under some sort of cover so that players do not see them. Examples:

a large nail	a pair of shoes
a box of matches	a tennis ball
bicycle clips	a potato
a plastic plate	a tambourine
a book	a knife and fork
a baking tin	a chain
a handful of marbles	a dart

ACTION

Give each player a pencil and some paper. Make sure that each person is sat with his back towards the group leader, who proceeds to drop the articles onto a table, one at a time. Each player writes down what he thinks is making the sound. If necessary, drop the articles twice. The player with the most correct answers is the winner.

VARIATIONS

Make a recording of various sounds. This could include a train, a car engine, running water, footsteps, crockery rattling, winding a clock, opening a newspaper, tearing paper, gargling and so on. The recording is played and participants write down their interpretation of the sound.

COMMENT

To make this game easier, give the players a list of items. As articles are dropped or the recording is played they must match the sound to the item. However, it is usually much more fun to give the players free imaginative flight.

FAMOUS PEOPLE

MATERIALS

None.

PREPARATION

None.

ACTION

Ask one member of the group to think of a famous person. This personality can be someone from any walk of life, past or present, the only criterion being that they are well known. The player then states whether the person he has thought of is 'alive or dead'. The remainder of the group now ask up to twenty questions in order to discover the famous personage. The questions can be answered only with a 'yes' or 'no'. Give points for players who can beat the group.

VARIATIONS

1   Use as a team game with players from one team trying to beat the opposing team.
2   Instead of a famous person, players think of a dream or fantasy. Examples might include: winning the pools, being prime minister for a week or landing on the moon. The other players ask twenty questions to discover the dream or fantasy.

COMMENT

A very useful, low-key game which is easy to organise. It can be used as a confidence-builder and to encourage participation.

POST-BOXES

MATERIALS

Cardboard boxes, paper and pencils.

PREPARATION

Label four, five or six cardboard boxes with town names, cut a post-box slit in the top or side and place in strategic points around the room. Also write the town names on slips of paper — one town on each. It does not matter how often each town is repeated.

ACTION

Decide on one place in the room which can be used as a sorting office. Each player goes to the sorting office to collect a slip of paper with a town name written on it. He then write his own name on it and 'posts' it in the appropriate post-box. Next he returns to the sorting office and queues for another slip. When all the pieces of paper in the sorting office have been posted, each box is checked. The player with the most correctly posted slips is the winner.

VARIATION

To simplify, or if the group is very large, divide the players into several teams. Each team member goes up in turn, collects a slip of paper, writes his team name on it, then posts it. When he has completed the procedure, the next team member goes to the sorting office and so on. The team with the most correctly posted slips wins.

COMMENT

Use well-known towns or local place-names for the post-boxes. Depending on the age and physical ability of the group, it may be desirable to rule that each player walks when posting the slips of paper.

PICTURE POSING

MATERIALS

Two chairs, pieces of paper and a bag.

PREPARATION

Think up a selection of situations or themes such as:

ballroom dancing	apathy
leaving home	joy
sailing	kindness
climbing	cruelty
skiing	obedience
on holiday	love
getting married	anger
on honeymoon	quarrelling
a christening	laziness

ACTION

Form the group into a circle and place two chairs in the centre. Ask for two volunteers. Now another person picks a theme or situation from the bag and poses the two volunteers for a picture, using the chairs as props. When the pose is complete he mimes taking their photograph and group members sitting in the circle then have to guess the theme. The photographer now takes the place of one of the two volunteers. Another person is invited to pick a theme from the bag and the procedure begins again.

COMMENT

A game to stimulate creative initiative and one which allows physical contact. Bear in mind that situations or activities are easier to pose than abstract themes.

ON THE MOVE

Exuberant games using vigorous movement

NEWSPAPER HOCKEY

MATERIALS

Old newspapers, sticky tape and a soft ball.

PREPARATION

Roll the sheets of newspaper to make hockey sticks.

ACTION

Divide the group members into two teams. Seat the teams on two rows of chairs facing each other, about three feet apart. Give each player a 'hockey stick'. Place chairs at each end of the rows for goal posts. Instruct players not to lift the hockey sticks above knee level. Put the ball in the centre and on the word 'go' or a whistle the teams bully off. Players must remain seated at all times. Change the direction of play at a pre-set time. The team scoring the most goals is the winner.

COMMENT

This is an exhilarating game during which players are liable to become very excited. To avoid bruised legs, be very strict about hockey sticks not being lifted higher than knee level and players remaining in their seats.

NUMBER FORMATIONS

MATERIALS

Card, string and a magic marker.

PREPARATION

Cut the card into pieces about six inches square. Sort the cards into sets of five (or whatever number is needed for equal teams) and number them one to five. Attach a piece of string to each card so that it can be hung round someone's neck.

ACTION

Form the players into teams and give each team a set of cards. Players hang the cards around their necks. Now call out numbers of up to five digits, using the numbers on the cards. (One to eight if there are eight players in each team.) The teams quickly form the number called out. The first team in the correct order wins a point. Then another number is called out. The game continues in this fashion.

VARIATIONS

Complicate the game by making players add, subtract, divide and multiply to arrive at a number.

COMMENT

If it is required to use 0, instruct the players to leave a space between each other. When asking players to add, subtract and so on, work out the sums before the game begins to ensure that the answers can be formed with the numbers on the players' cards.

PASS THE BALL

MATERIALS

Two balls.

PREPARATION

None.

ACTION

Split the group into two teams and have opposing players sit in a line facing each other. Ask the first player in each team to extend his legs, keeping his ankles together. Place a ball on each pair of extended ankles. The balls must now be transferred to the next person in the team, using legs only. If a ball is dropped, it must go back to the beginning again. The first team successful in getting their ball to the end and back again is the winner.

VARIATIONS

Place the ball under the first player's chin. It is then passed to the next player, who holds it under his chin. The use of hands is not allowed. As an alternative to having two teams, the ball can be passed around a circle in this manner. Also, instead of a ball, use an orange or a matchbox.

COMMENT

This is an excellent touching game. It is a good idea to ask players to remove their shoes before the game starts. People who do not like being touched may find the variation difficult. It is better to lead up to it with less threatening touch games. Try to place tall and short, thin and fat people next to each other.

GONE SHOPPING

MATERIALS

Paper, magic marker and Blu-Tack.

PREPARATION

Prepare large sheets of paper with types of shops written across them in bold letters. Examples:

florist	pet shop	grocer
restaurant	garage	butcher
newsagent	post office	office supplies

Write a list of at least twelve articles each shop sells under the bold printing.

ACTION

Stick the sheets of paper up in different parts of the room. Ask players to walk freely around the room. After a moment call out for everyone to buy a particular article. People must queue up in front of the correct shop. Anyone not in the right queue is 'out'. Occasionally, call out an item which cannot be purchased in any of the shops. Any players who queue up then are also 'out'.

COMMENT

A quick thinking game which is relatively easy to play and one which provides a great deal of fun.

MUSICAL ISLANDS

MATERIALS

Record-player, records and sheets of newspaper.

PREPARATION

None.

ACTION

Place sheets taken from newspapers around the room on the floor. Ask players to walk around the room while music is played. When it stops participants rush to a newspaper sheet and crowd onto it. Anyone not on a sheet or falling off is out of the game. Keep reducing the sheets so that at least one player is out each time. Also fold the sheets so that they are smaller and more difficult to stand on.

VARIATIONS

1 Musical patterns. The players are split into groups of six to eight people. While music is played, they walk around the room, intermingling. When the music stops, the leader calls out a pattern, such as: a square, a triangle, a diamond, an octagon, the letter A or the letter O. Players must assemble with other members of their group and form the shape of the pattern. Team points can be awarded for the first team to complete each pattern.

2 Musical objects. Balls or other objects are placed around the room. While music is played people walk around the room. When it stops, players dash to grab one of the objects. When the music restarts they must put the object back and begin walking again. If desired, the number of objects can be gradually reduced and players eliminated.

COMMENT

Always enjoyable. The music creates an atmosphere of fun. Depending on the physical abilities of group members, it may be advisable to insist that players walk, rather than run.

ALL CHANGE!

MATERIALS

None.

PREPARATION

None.

ACTION

Ask players to choose a partner. If there is an odd number, the person who is left over can be the leader. Partners face each other and the leader calls out commands such as:

"Stand back to back!"   "Shake hands!"

"Hold hands!"   "Make funny faces!"

"Link arms!"   "Stand on one leg!"

After a pre-set time, or when he chooses, the leader commands: "All change!" Now each player must find a new partner. The leader also tries to find a partner. Whoever is left surplus becomes the leader and calls out the commands.

VARIATION

Military parade. Form the players into a military formation of three in a line. The leader calls out military commands like:

"Quick march!"   "Left turn!"   "Right wheel!"

"Halt!"   "Salute!"   "Slow march!"

"Right turn!"   "Left wheel!"   "Double march!"

Anyone not complying or seen to be doing the wrong action becomes the leader.

COMMENT

The commands can include vigorous movements and exercises or, alternatively, adopt a more gentle approach, according to the requirements and mood of the group.

MATERIALS

None.

PREPARATION

Prepare a list, or lists, of obstacles such as a swamp infested with crocodiles; a river; minefields; high fences; wild animals; hostile natives.

ACTION

Split the group into teams. Explain that each team has been trapped and left in a locked hut in the jungle. They have only a rope, a ladder and a table to use to escape. There are a number of obstacles between them and freedom. Each team then plans their escape.

After ten minutes or so, the teams take it in turn to act out their escape for everyone else to see. Finally, have each member state what he would like most when he had made good his escape. This might be a drink of water, a hot bath, a beer, to see someone special and so on.

When teams have enacted the escapes, have a general discussion on whether or not each member would have survived a real escape in a similar situation. How would they cope?

VARIATIONS

1 Give each team a different situation from which to escape. Examples:
   a) Escape from an enemy country.
   b) Escape from a lonely country house.
   c) Escape from a multi-storey building which is on fire.

   Vary the articles the group are allowed with which to make good their escape and also the obstacles. Make them appropriate to the situation.

2 To add variety, present each individual with a different situation, different obstacles and different tools and have him plan his escape.

COMMENT

This game can be played for fun only, or angled to enable follow-up discussion of real-life emergencies: what to do in case of fire, flooding, electricity being cut off, accidents and so on.

ODDS AND EVENS

MATERIALS

Cardboard, string and a magic marker.

PREPARATION

Cut the cardboard into six-inch squares. Make up the same number of cards as there are players and number them one to twenty or whatever it might be. Attach a piece of string to each card so that it can be hung around someone's neck.

ACTION

Divide the group into two teams and seat them facing each other. Give one team all the odd-numbered cards and the other team the cards with even numbers. Players memorise their numbers, then hang the cards around their necks. Now call out two numbers, one odd, one even. The people wearing these numbers walk or run — according to instructions — around the line of chairs and back to their places. The first person back scores a point for his team. Another two numbers are called out and so on.

VARIATIONS

Complicate matters by calling out the numbers in a cryptic manner. Examples:

1 — first, or top dog.

2 — duet, or eyes.

3 — triplets or tripod.

4 — quads, or Just Men.

5 — toes on one foot, or one more than four.

6 — half a dozen, or twelve divided by two.

7 — deadly sins, or the number of seas.

8 — ten minus two, or twice four.

Allow the teams to help individual players to work out the answers.

COMMENT

To introduce the game, begin by calling out the numbers and then make it more difficult by moving into the cryptic format. It is, of course, prudent to have the clues prepared before the game starts.

FAN THE BALLOON

MATERIALS

Newspapers, balloons and chalk.

PREPARATION

Blow up the balloons.

ACTION

Form the group into teams. Draw a line some twelve to fifteen feet away from the first player in each team. Place a balloon on the floor in front of the team leaders and give them a newspaper. They must now fan the balloons to the line and back. The second player in each team does likewise and so the game continues until everyone has fanned the balloon. The first team finished is the winner.

VARIATIONS

1 Instead of a newspaper use a brush. Players have to sweep the balloon to the line and back again.
2 Standing behind a line each player throws a balloon as far as possible. Mark the spots with chalk or matchsticks. This is more difficult with shaped balloons.
3 Tie a balloon to each player's ankle and give them a rolled-up newspaper each. The object is to burst as many opponents' balloons as possible, using only the rolled-up newspapers. When a player's balloon is burst, that player is out. The last player left with his balloon intact wins.

COMMENT

Balloons give a jolly atmosphere and bring out a sense of fun in people.

GOING THROUGH THE MOTIONS

MATERIALS

None.

PREPARATION

None.

ACTION

Form the group into a circle. Start the game by performing an action, or have a player think of one. This could be tapping your foot. The player next to you then repeats the movement you performed and adds one of his own. The third player now does the first two actions, plus a third. This continues on around the circle until everyone has added a movement.

VARIATION

It helps other players to remember, and can be more fun, if all the players who have performed an action do all the movements together each time. Then the person whose turn it is adds his own. Eventually, everyone is in motion together.

COMMENT

Movements can be kept simple or made more energetic. This is a good memory exercise.

OBSTACLE COURSE

MATERIALS

Chairs, or other items which can be used as obstacles, and blindfolds.

PREPARATION

Prepare a series of obstacles which will obstruct players as they walk across the room in a straight line.

ACTION

Ask for two volunteers. One person is blindfolded. The other player, giving only verbal instruction, now guides his partner across the room and around the obstacles. Once across the room, the person who was blindfolded becomes the guide for the return journey. When the course has been completed, another two players have a go. The players who cross the room and return in the quickest time can be acclaimed the winners.

VARIATIONS

1   To make this game more difficult, turn the blindfolded player around three times before he commences the journey. Also move the obstacles about after the blindfold has been applied.
2   Have several couples crossing the room in different directions at the same time. Amid all the noise and various shouted commands there is a tendency to follow wrong instructions.

COMMENT

A good trust exercise. Unless players are confident, it is better to begin the game gently and work up to the more difficult variations.

BIRTHDAY MIME

MATERIALS

None.

PREPARATION

None.

ACTION

Ask group members to think about the month in which they were born. What happens during that time which is associated with the month? Give time to think and then have each person do a mime to represent the event. Other group members try to guess what the event is and the month in which the person was born.

VARIATIONS

1   Do a 'seasons' mime, using autumn, winter, spring and summer. Let members think up their own associated events or provide them on slips of paper and have players select one from a bag.
2   Have players mime something beginning with the first letter of the month in which they were born.
3   Players mime some event associated with a specific year. Year and event can be provided on slips of paper to be chosen from a bag, or people can recall an event for themselves.

COMMENT

A trip to the library to look at a book of dates or a history book will provide plenty of events associated with specific years. Old newspapers are another good source.

POTATO RACE

MATERIALS

Potatoes, a broad-bladed knife, a bowl and two chairs.

PREPARATION

None.

ACTION

Place a chair with a potato on it at one end of the room and another chair with a bowl on it at the other. Give the first player a knife and instruct him to lift the potato with the knife, carry it the length of the room and deposit it in the bowl. If he drops or touches it he must start again. He is not allowed to stick the knife into the potato. When one player has succeeded, invite others to have a turn.

VARIATION

Divide the group into teams. The first team finished is the winner.

COMMENT

To make the game easier, use a tennis ball and racket.

BLIND RACE

MATERIALS

Blindfolds, boxes, balls or other objects such as potatoes.

PREPARATION

None.

ACTION

Have three or four players each stand at one end of the room by an empty box or bowl with a partner. Four balls are placed at intervals in front of them. One player is blindfolded and, under instructions called out by his partner who must remain by the box, walks to the first ball, returns and places it in the box. This continues until all four balls are in the box.

VARIATION

Use as a team game. The first team to finish is the winner.

COMMENT

It is inadvisable to have more than four pairs playing at once as the confusion from the commands becomes too much. Lots of concentration and trust is needed when playing this game. If having several pairs working together is too threatening, start by using only one couple.

MAIL ROBBER

MATERIALS

Blindfold, card and string.

PREPARATION

Write the names of towns on cards. Attach string, so the cards can be hung round players' necks.

ACTION

Sit the players in a fairly wide circle. Ask one person to volunteer to sit outside and another player to stand in the centre of the circle. The person in the centre, the mail robber, is blindfolded and the people sat in the circle are given cards with town names which are hung around their necks. The person outside the circle now calls out two of the town names. The players with these cards must exchange places. They may tiptoe or run. The person in the centre, the mail robber, tries to intercept by catching one of the two players changing places. When he does, that person then becomes the mail robber.

COMMENT

To avoid roughness, have 'touching' the criterion, rather than grabbing. Also give other players an opportunity to call out the town names.

MIMING TO MUSIC

MATERIALS

Record-player and records.

PREPARATION

None.

ACTION

Stand in the centre of the room or on a platform at one end where everyone can see and hear you. Have music playing in the background. Start everyone walking freely around the room. After a lap or two ask them to swim around the room. Everyone now mimes swimming motions as they move. Continue in this manner, changing the ways of moving around the room. Here are some more suggestions:

running	skipping	slowly
jumping	hopping	drunkenly
riding	tiptoeing	happily
flying	sideways	proudly
dancing	skating	hurriedly
backwards	limping	lazily

VARIATIONS

1 Divide the members into groups and number the groups one to three or whatever it might be. Then tell all the 'ones' to go round the room in a specific way, 'twos' to go round in another way and 'threes' yet another. Every so often, call out one of the numbers and alter the way that group is walking.

2 As for variation one above but have only one group do a movement and return to base. Another number is called out and this group does a movement and returns to its base. And so it continues.

3 Start the group walking around the room and invent an action story which connects action movements.
   Here is an example:
'Tom walked slowly through the forest. Dawn was breaking. Suddenly, he heard a noise. A twig snapping. He stopped. What

was it? A predator in the forest. Tom walked on hurriedly. He heard it again. Panicking, he ran and ran and ran and ran until he came to a river. The sound behind was coming nearer, and getting louder. He jumped into the river and began to swim hurriedly towards the other side . . .'

And so on. The players perform the actions as the story is told. There is no need to keep the story-line logical, but do try to create atmosphere with tone of voice. It is better to write down some sort of story-line or a list of actions, so that things can be kept going.

COMMENT

This game can be enjoyed by players of all ages as the actions can be varied to suit. Use bright, energetic music. Also give players a chance to call out changes in movements or to make up the story. Have one player start the story, another carry on, and so on.

TOUCH SENSE

MATERIALS

Blindfolds.

PREPARATION

None.

ACTION

Have players walk slowly around the room with their eyes closed or wearing blindfolds. Post non-players on each side of the room to ensure that no one trips up or walks into anything. Players reach out and touch things: curtains, the walls, the door, the windows and so on, but have to avoid other people. After a brief time, the leader tells everyone to reach out and find a partner. Anyone who has difficulty finding someone can be guided by a non-player. Everyone now touches his partner, feeling his hands, face and hair. By using touch only, they try to guess the name of the other person. After a while everyone is instructed to start walking again for a bit and then to find another partner. And so the game continues.

VARIATIONS

1 Have one blindfolded player in the centre of a circle. Turn him around a few times, or have the other players change places. The blindfolded person is then guided up to someone. He feels the person's hands, face and hair and tries to guess who it is. After a few tries have been made at identifying various players, someone else is blindfolded and has a turn.

2 People from various origins and backgrounds greet each other differently. Some shake hands, some embrace, some kiss the hands of the female sex, some rub noses or kiss each other on the cheek. Pair members up and have each pair think up a new greeting. Each couple then demonstrates this greeting to the group. It can be as silly as they wish. Examples might be: shaking both hands at once while standing on one leg, or standing back-to-back and shaking hands over their heads.

COMMENT

While the blindfolded walk is going on, it is helpful to the less confident if you keep a commentary going while they are walking. You can say things like: "Be aware of sounds. Feel the texture of things. Are there empty spaces around you? Can you feel the presence of someone close by? Is he short or tall?"

The sound of your voice will help those who are timid and unsure. It reminds them that you are watching and that no harm will come to them.

WOLF

MATERIALS

None.

PREPARATION

None.

ACTION

Seat half the players in a circle. Have one empty chair. The other players now stand behind the chairs with their hands behind their backs. The person who is stood behind the empty chair is known as 'wolf'. He winks at one of the seated people who tries to escape and run to sit on the empty chair. The player standing behind the escapee should attempt to stop him getting away by grabbing him by the shoulders. If he fails, he then becomes the 'wolf'. After a pre-set time or when everyone has had a chance to escape, change the players over, so that those standing become the seated players.

COMMENT

Add to the game by having forfeits for abortive attempts at escape. Let the person standing behind the escapee's chair think of the penalty, such as reciting a nursery rhyme, telling a joke or doing a physical exercise.

SIMON SAYS

MATERIALS

None.

PREPARATION

None.

ACTION

This game can be performed with the players seated or standing. One person gives the commands. He may call out: "Simon says 'Scratch your head!'" Everyone carries out the action. Next he could command: "Stand on one foot!" If he gives an order without the prefix 'Simon says' and players carry out the action, they are out of the game. The object is to catch as many people out as possible. When only one person is left doing the actions, let him have a turn at giving the orders.

VARIATIONS

'Do this, do that'. The rules are the same as for 'Simon says', except that the leader performs an action saying: "Do this" or "Do that". When he says, "Do this" the players perform the action, when he says, "Do that", they refrain.

COMMENT

As well as providing exercise, which can be as gentle or as vigorous as required, this game is good for quick thinking and concentration. Encourage the leader to call out the commands in quick succession.

SQUARE PITCH

MATERIALS

A large piece of card, a magic marker, a ruler, coloured pencils or paints and some small coins or flat discs.

PREPARATION

Rule out nine squares on the piece of cardboard as shown in *Figure 4.1*. Number the squares. Colouring can be used to good effect — one colour to a square.

6	2	4
8	1	7
5	9	3

Figure 4.1

ACTION

Lay the board on the floor. Players pitch coins or flat discs from about seven or eight feet away. Coins landing on lines do not count as a score. The first player to reach a pre-set target, say one hundred, is the winner.

VARIATIONS

Instead of a square, use a target as shown in *Figure 4.2*.

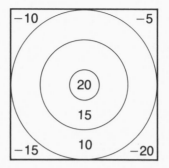

Figure 4.2

COMMENT

This game is ideal for running a short tournament using several boards. Pair players off, or divide them into small groups so that each player gets an opportunity to play every other player. The person who wins the most games is the overall winner.

SOLVE A PROBLEM

Games using puzzles and brain-teasers

ODD MAN OUT

MATERIALS

Pencils and paper.

PREPARATION

None.

ACTION

Form the players into two or more teams. Instruct the teams to make up ten lists of four, five or six words with one word being the odd man out. Here is an example:

Fiat	Jaguar	Mercedes
Ford	Limousine	Volvo

'Limousine' is the odd word out: it relates to cars of a type, the others are specific makes of car. When the lists have been compiled, an elected leader from each team takes turns at calling out one of the word groups. The opposing teams have ten or fifteen seconds to name the odd word out and state why it is odd. And so the game continues until all ten lists from each team have been called out. Allow points to teams for discovering the odd man out and also for presenting a list which beats the other teams.

COMMENT

Lists of words can be supplied, saving the players the task of having to make up the puzzles. To make the composing of lists easier, stipulate only four words in each group. Alternatively, make the game more difficult by increasing the number of words on each list — make it seven or eight. This is a good game for group interaction, inspiring team work and stimulating quick thinking.

PASS THE PROVERB

MATERIALS

Pencils and paper.

PREPARATION

Jot down a list of proverbs equal to the number of players in the group and number them, one to twelve, or whatever it might be. Next, write the proverbs on separate pieces of paper with the letters in each word close together but omitting the vowels. For example, the proverb: 'Better bend than break', would become; 'BTTR BND THN BRK'. Number each piece of paper to correspond with the original list.

ACTION

Seat the group in a circle. Give each player a sheet of paper and a pencil. Ask everyone to write the numbers down the left-hand side of the paper. Now hand out a proverb to each player. Everyone tries to decipher the proverb they have been given, then writes it down. After about two minutes, yell "Change!". Each player must pass his proverb on to his neighbour. The procedure continues until all the players have seen every proverb. If you wish, allow a few minutes at the end for players to call out the numbers and have a second look at proverbs they were unable to decipher. Lastly, have players call out what they have written down for each proverb and correct as necessary. The person who has deciphered the most is the winner.

VARIATIONS

Instead of proverbs use well-known quotations, titles of books, famous people and so on.

COMMENT

To make the game more difficult, run the words in the proverb together. The above example would then look like this: 'BTTRBNDTHNBRK'.

MATERIALS

Card, paper, magic marker, glue and scissors.

PREPARATION

Draw a grid, using the magic marker, as in *Figure 5.1* or *5.2*. Fill in words which fit across the grid and make a separate list of clues to each word. When this is completed, photocopy the grid and paste each copy onto thin card. Cut each card into squares, each square containing a letter. Make up several sets of letters in this fashion.

1	L	O	O	T
2	R	A	I	N
3	C	A	R	T
4	F	E	E	L

CLUES
1 Illicit gains.
2 Small drops of water.
3 A horse-drawn carriage.
4 Touch.

Figure 5.1

1	S	A	I	L	O	R
2	R	E	D	U	C	E
3	L	A	W	Y	E	R
4	T	O	M	A	T	O
5	F	O	L	L	O	W
6	P	R	O	F	I	T

CLUES
1 A seaman.
2 To make smaller.
3 A member of the legal profession.
4 A red fruit.
5 To come after.
6 Gain.

Figure 5.2

ACTION

Split the group into teams and give each team a set of letters. Draw a blank grid on a blackboard or a large sheet of paper and write the clues alongside. Each team proceeds to put the letters together forming the words in the correct order.

VARIATIONS

Make these puzzles up using the names of famous people or countries, cities and so on.

COMMENT

The puzzles can be made short and simple by using four- or five-letter words, or more complex by using six-, seven- or eight-letter words. The clues given can be made easy or difficult.

FIND THE CHANGE

MATERIALS

None.

PREPARATION

None.

ACTION

Split the players into two teams and line them up facing each other. Instruct the participants to have a good look at the person opposite them. Allow one to two minutes, then have everyone turn round so that the teams are back to back. Request that each player changes three things about his appearance. This could be undoing a shirt button, taking off a ring, loosening a tie and so on. When the changes have been made, ask the teams to turn about again and face the same player as before. Now see if each player is observant enough to notice what his opposing team member has changed about his appearance. The team with the most correct answers wins.

VARIATION

Have the players sit in a circle. One participant is studied, then leaves the room to change three items of his appearance. When he returns everyone tries to guess what alterations have been made. Let each person in the group have a turn and see who can outwit the rest.

COMMENT

A game which can be played with subtlety or in an obvious manner, making it suitable for all to play. It is useful as a memory and observation exercise.

TRUE OR FALSE?

MATERIALS

Pencils and paper.

PREPARATION

None.

ACTION

Divide the players into two teams. Instruct each team to make up — according to the number of players in the team — a list of statements which may be true or false. A statement could be: 'Sap rises up the tree in the spring and falls again in autumn.' When teams have completed the lists players take turns at making their statements. The opposing players state whether it is true or false and why. In the example given the answer might be: 'It is false. Sap moves from the centre of the tree to the bark and back — not up and down.' The team with the most correct answers wins.

VARIATIONS

1 Teams tell 'tall' stories or personal anecdotes of bravery, things they have done or achieved. The opposing team have to guess whether each story is true or false.
2 Give each team a book of quotations or proverbs. The players then make up some quotations and include some which are true. The opposing teams have to state which are true and which false.

COMMENT

Players can be seated in a circle and encouraged to think up individual statements, anecdotes or stories. However, it is usually easier and less stressful to participants when teams are formed.

JOINING UP

MATERIALS

Pencils and paper.

PREPARATION

Make out two lists of part words. For example:

List 1	List 2	Answers
ENT	BON	CARBON
PUR	SON	PERSON
GUN	ADE	PARADE
MAN	HER	FATHER
PAT	TER	LETTER
BAL	RED	HATRED
OPP	NEL	KENNEL
RUN	UCE	REDUCE
SET	STY	SUNDRY
BAD	DRY	AMBUSH
CRU	USH	CRUSTY
AMB	TEE	BADGER
SUN	GER	SETTEE
KEN	AGE	RUNNER
LET	ENT	PATENT
CAR	NER	OPPOSE
FAT	OSE	MANAGE
PAR	ICE	GUNNER
RED	LET	ENTICE
HAT	NER	BALLET
PER	EST	PUREST

ACTION

Split the group into teams, hand out paper and pencils and see which team is the quickest to make up the complete words.

VARIATIONS

Make similar lists of authors, film stars, sports personalities, historical figures and so on, using forenames for one list and surnames for the other.

COMMENT

Individuals can complete the list on their own. It may be a good idea to have an allotted time in which to complete the puzzle. A list of about twenty words is usually adequate.

DESCRIBING THE OBJECT

MATERIALS

A bag and a number of objects such as a damp sponge, a toy car, a leather comb case, a pen, an empty milk bottle or a piece of fruit.

PREPARATION

None.

ACTION

Seat the group in a circle. Have the objects in a separate room or behind a screen of some sort. Unseen by the group, place one of the objects in the bag. Ask one player to place his hands behind his back. Hold the bag so the object cannot be seen by the player or anyone else. Keeping his hands behind his back the player places his hands inside the bag and feels the object. After a few seconds he begins to describe it, giving the size, shape, texture and so on. He is not allowed to state what he thinks it is. The group must guess from the description being given. When it has been guessed, go behind the screen, remove the item and replace it with something else. Another player now has a turn at describing the object. And so the game continues.

COMMENT

A game which provides fun and makes people more aware of the sense of touch. It also helps to inspire imaginative descriptive powers.

FEELY BAGS

MATERIALS

A magic marker, cloth material and about twenty-four small household objects such as a piece of coal, a dog biscuit, a cotton reel, a curtain hook, a hair curler, a screw, a pencil-sharpener and so forth. Pencils and paper are also required.

PREPARATION

Cut out and sew up twenty-four bags about three to four inches square, each to contain one object. Number the bags clearly with a magic marker, one to twenty-four and make a note of the objects to correspond with the numbers.

ACTION

Seat the group in a circle and give each person a pencil and a piece of paper. Ask everyone to write the numbers one to twenty-four down the left-hand side of the paper. When this has been done, give out the feely bags and ask players to write down what they think is inside each bag before passing it on to their neighbour. When everyone has had an opportunity to feel all the bags, have players call out what they think is in them. The person with the most correct answers is the winner.

COMMENT

Another game which is excellent for interaction and initiating involvement. People cannot resist having a go and exchanging opinions on what is in the bags. It is also a game which can be kept and used time and time again.

BLANK PUZZLE

MATERIALS

Pencils and paper.

PREPARATION

None.

ACTION

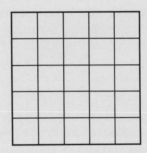

Figure 5.3

Instruct each player to draw a block of squares on a piece of paper as shown in *Figure 5.3*. Then have players call out a letter of the alphabet in turn. As letters are called, all the players must put that letter in a square. The object is to fill the squares with letters, reading from left to right and top to bottom, to make complete words. When a player has a turn at calling out a letter, he chooses the letter most useful to him. Each letter called must be inserted in a blank square, otherwise there will be blank squares left when all twenty-five letters have been called out. Two-letter words do not count and proper names are not allowed. Players score points for the words formed — a point for each letter in the word. Words within words do not count and a point can be subtracted for each blank square.

COMMENT

Quick thinking and concentration are needed for this game. It also ensures participation by all players. For the really enthusiastic, lengthen the game time by increasing the number of squares to accommodate six- or even eight-letter words. If you do this, disallow the use of two-, three- or even four-letter words when scoring. The game can also be made shorter by reducing the number of squares to sixteen.

TOWNS AND CITIES

MATERIALS

Pencils and paper.

PREPARATION

Draw a map of the country, marking well-known towns and cities on it with numbered blobs. Do not write the name of the town or city on the map. A list of these is then written at the bottom of the sheet. Ensure that they are not numbered in the same sequence as they are on the map. Produce as many copies as necessary to give one to each player. Making the map small enough to fit on an A4 size sheet facilitates photocopying.

ACTION

Give out the blank maps and ask the players to write the names of the cities and towns by the correct blob. When everyone has completed the task ask players to call out what they have written down for town number one. If necessary correct the answer and continue in the same fashion through the rest. The player with the most correct is the winner.

VARIATIONS

1   Substitute counties for towns and cities. Show the county bound-aries on the map and number each county. List the counties at the bottom of the sheet.
2   Draw a map of Europe showing the country boundaries and number each country. List the countries at the bottom of the sheet.
3   Draw a map of America showing state boundaries and number each state. List the states at the bottom of the sheet.

COMMENT

Develop the exercise by having a short discussion about each town as it is called out. Let players comment on their impressions and memories of particular places.

FOLLOW THE NUMBER

MATERIALS

Pencils and paper.

PREPARATION

Think up sets of numbers in a specific order, leaving the last two numbers blank. For example:

60	50	40	30	——	(20	10)
15	30	60	120	——	(240	480)
13	14	16	19	——	(23	28)
2	6	18	54	——	(162	486)
25	30	35	40	——	(45	50)
100	99	97	94	——	(90	85)

ACTION

Have participants write the numbers down, give them prepared sheets or write the puzzle up on a blackboard. The players enter the numbers which have been omitted.

COMMENT

More complex number patterns can be worked out to include division, square roots and so on.

STEPPING-STONES

MATERIALS

Pencils and paper.

PREPARATION

Think up several sets of category or theme words. Alternatively, start the game by having group members call out a number of them. Examples:

1 Music	Animals	Gardening	Famous people
2 Theatre	Sport	Farming	Cars
3 Cookery	Astronomy	Dancing	Finance
4 Wildlife	Photography	Drawing	Sailing
5 Crime	Education	Politics	Racing

ACTION

Form the group into teams. Ask each team to string up to nine phrases, statements or sentences together in order to get from the first category word to the last. Each statement must touch on the themes in the order given, using them as stepping-stones. If example number one above was used, a team might come up with:

Andrew Lloyd Webber is a composer. (Music)

He composed the musical 'Cats'. (Animals)

Cats are animals which like large gardens to roam in.

If you have a large garden it is difficult to keep it well cultivated. (Gardening)

The gardens of famous people are often featured in magazines. (Famous people)

When each team has completed the task the statements are read out. Opposing teams must agree that all the themes have been touched upon and that nothing is too far-fetched.

COMMENT

To make the game more difficult, have more than four theme words in each set. Once players are confident and familiar with the game they can play individually rather than in teams.

TASTE TEST

MATERIALS

Drinking glasses, an assortment of drinks, blindfolds, pencils and paper.

PREPARATION

Make a list of the drinks, which may be cold tea, lemonade, water, lemon juice, blackcurrant drink, tonic water and so on.

ACTION

Line players up outside an adjacent room or in front of some sort of screen. Blindfold each person in turn, lead him into the room and give him a sip from a glass. He is then led back again and the blindfold removed so that he can write down what he thought he was drinking. This continues until everyone has tasted drink number one. To speed things up two or three people can be guided into the room at the same time. Follow the same procedure until all the drinks have been tasted. Then sit everyone down in a circle and see how many people have correctly identified what they were drinking.

VARIATIONS

1   Half fill clear jars with items such as peas, matches, biscuits, pins, marbles, stones, beads and coins. Players have to guess how many there are of the items. The person nearest to the number in each case is awarded points.
2   Place a number of strong smelling items in jam jars which have been wrapped with paper or cloth, numbered and with holes pricked in the metal tops. Have players guess what is in the jars by smelling.
3   Record the voices of famous people from the radio and television. Play them to the group and ask participants to identify them.

COMMENT

These are puzzle games in which everyone can compete with a sense of fun. They initiate good interaction.

FIND THE MAXIM

MATERIALS

Pencils and paper.

PREPARATION

A list of maxims such as:

1 Too many cooks spoil the broth.
2 Don't count your chickens before they're hatched.
3 Look before you leap.
4 Don't put all your eggs in one basket.
5 Pride goes before a fall.
6 Don't judge a book by its cover.

ACTION

Divide the players into two teams. Give each group a different maxim written on a piece of paper or have them think of one themselves. Simultaneously, both teams then compose sentences which contain one word from the maxim. An example might be:

Maxim: Many hands make light work. Sentences:

How *many* people were there?

Peter is clever with his *hands*.

I know how to *make* it squeak.

There is a *light* on in your room.

I start *work* at nine o'clock.

Both teams list their sentences on sheets of paper which are then exchanged. Set a time-limit. The first team to find the hidden maxim and shout it out wins five points. The opposition still receive two points if they beat the time-limit. Continue the game by repeating the procedure. The team with the most points at the end of the session is the winner.

COMMENT

If the group is very big, divide it into several small groups of two, three or four people. Each group then thinks of a maxim and the sentences. When this has been completed each group takes a turn at presenting sentences to all the other players, who try to find the maxim.

SPOT THE DIFFERENCE

MATERIALS

Card, pencils, paper and scissors.

PREPARATION

Draw or trace a picture. Cartoon pictures are excellent for this game. Reproduce the same picture but this time change ten details. Leave a few things out and add other detail. Take three or four photocopies of both pictures. Paste the pictures with the changed details onto thin card and cut into a puzzle — say twelve pieces.

ACTION

Divide the group into three or four teams. Give each team a complete picture, accompanied by the pieces of the second picture with the alterations. On the word 'go' the teams put the puzzle picture together and try to spot the differences. After a pre-set time or when one team finishes stop the proceedings. Have teams call out the differences in turn and see which team has correctly spotted the most.

COMMENT

Make the game easier by using simple drawings containing less detail. A good game for observation, it encourages people to work together and promotes interaction.

CATEGORIES

MATERIALS

Pencils and paper.

PREPARATION

None.

ACTION

Have the players decide on about ten categories. Each person writes these down in a list as shown in *Figure 5.4*, column 1. Someone then chooses a letter of the alphabet. Players think of a word beginning with that letter for each category and then write it down as in column 2. Each person tries to think of unusual words which none of the others will have chosen. When everyone has completed the list, or an allotted time is up, players call out their words. Ten points can be awarded for words not used by other players and five points when two or more people have the same word. Once players have counted up their scores and a winner has been established, another letter of

	C	P	S
FISH	cod	pike	
FLOWERS	carnation	primrose	
CITIES	Copenhagen	Prague	
VEGETABLES	cucumber	parsnip	
COUNTRIES	Cyprus	Poland	
ANIMALS	cow	pony	
COLOURS	cream	pink	
BIRDS	curlew	pigeon	
BOYS' NAMES	Charles	Peter	
GIRLS' NAMES	Charlotte	Patricia	
Column 1	Column 2	Column 3	Column 4

Figure 5.4

the alphabet can be called out. Players now write down words beginning with that letter for each category as in column 3. And so the game continues, for as many rounds as seems desirable.

COMMENT

Categories can be made simple by choosing easy themes such as colours, flowers and so on, or more difficult by selecting categories like chemicals, politicians or explorers. Easy or difficult letters of the alphabet may also be chosen. For example, W or J will be much more difficult than S or A. The category lists can be prepared beforehand and photocopied, so that sheets are ready to be handed out to the group.

CRAMBO

MATERIALS

None.

PREPARATION

None.

ACTION

Form the group into two teams. Ask one team, team 'A', to leave the room. The remainder of the group, team 'B', choose a word and decide on a second word which rhymes with the first. An example might be 'expression' and 'confession'. Bring team 'A' back into the room and tell them the word which rhymes with the first word chosen — in the above case, 'confession'. They must guess, without actually stating the word, other words which rhyme with the given word until the original word chosen is found out. To continue the example:

Team A   Would it be given on a first meeting with someone?

Team B   It is not impression.

Team A   Is it the name given to the length of time this group meets?

Team B   No, it is not session.

Team A   Is it something to sit on or support your back?

Team B   It is not cushion.

The procedure continues thus until team 'A' discovers the word or gives in. Team 'B' then leaves the room while team 'A' thinks of a word and another to rhyme with it. Award points for successful guesses and points to the opposing team when the word is not discovered.

VARIATIONS

1   Dumb Crambo. The procedure is the same, except that the players trying to guess the word are not allowed to speak — they must mime what they think the word is. If the mime is not correct, or not understood, the other team boos or hisses, if correct they applaud. If a player on the guessing team speaks, his team loses a point.

2   Seat the players in a circle. One player thinks of a word and then tells everyone a word which rhymes with it. For example: the word originally thought of might be 'bull' and the word which

rhymes with it 'pull'. The other players try to guess the original word.

COMMENT

The game can be played with individual players leaving the room. This, however, places a lot of pressure on one person. Also note that variation two is a simplified version of the game.

MEMORY BAG

MATERIALS

A cloth or plastic bag and about ten small household items such as a sponge, a knife, a ring, a plug, a shoehorn and so on. Make them relatively easy items to identify. Pencils and paper are also required.

PREPARATION

None.

ACTION

Seat the group in a circle and then pass the bag from person to person giving time for each individual to have a good feel of the contents. When everyone has done so, relieve them of the bag, hand out pencils and paper and ask them to write down all the items they can remember. Then go round the group and have each member call out one item he has noted down. As it is called, take the object out of the bag and show it to everyone. Finally, have players count up how many items they have remembered.

VARIATION

Place about fifteen objects on a tray and cover with a cloth. Remove the cloth for a moment so that the players can see what is on the tray and replace the cloth. Give everyone a pencil and a piece of paper to write down all the objects they can remember.

COMMENT

While the memory bag is being passed around, players will be tempted to make comments on the contents. To make the game more difficult have a rule that people must not reveal what they think is in the bag. This is an excellent memory game and can be concluded by discussing various ways of remembering things.

ACROSTICS

MATERIALS

Pencils and paper.

PREPARATION

None.

ACTION

Have the players call out a word and instruct them to write the letters down and up the page in the manner shown for the word 'energy':

```
E       Y
N       G
E       R
R       E
G       N
Y       E
```

Now divide the group into small teams. Each team must think up different words beginning and ending with the above letters. The more difficult and obscure the words the better. When this is completed, a player from one team — team 'A' — describes or gives a clue to the first word and the opposing teams try to guess what it is. The first team to guess scores a point. Provided no other team has thought of the same word the team — team 'A' — also scores a point. Then another team gives a clue to their first word. And so the game continues. The team with the most points at the end wins.

VARIATION

Have individual players compete. Award ten points for each word that no other player has thought of and five points for all other words.

COMMENT

If there are a lot of players or teams, limit the words chosen to start the game to between five and eight letters, otherwise the game will take a very long time.

MATERIALS

Pencils and paper.

PREPARATION

Draw a blank grid and write the name of a poet, reading downwards as shown in the first column of *Figure 5.5.* Now think up words beginning with each letter of the poet's name, reading across. Next, make a list of clues. Finally, draw another blank grid with the clues written alongside and the squares not used for letters blanked out. This can be photocopied.

1	J	O	I	N	E	R
2	O	R	D	E	R	
3	H	O	N	E	S	T
4	N	U	R	S	E	R	Y
5	K	E	N	N	E	L
6	E	V	E	N	T	
7	A	D	O	R	E	
8	T	H	E	R	M	
9	S	C	R	E	A	M

CLUES
1 Someone who makes furniture.
2 Command.
3 Righteous.
4 A place for children.
5 Home for an animal.
6 Occasion.
7 Worship.
8 Unit of heat.
9 A shrill cry.

Figure 5.5

ACTION

Divide the group into small teams. Either hand out the blank grids or draw it on the blackboard with the clues and have players make their own copies. The teams are to compete to see who will be the first to discover the poet.

VARIATIONS

1 Have the teams make up their own puzzles in the same manner and challenge each other.
2 Allow individuals to work on their own to find the poet.
3 Instead of poets use countries, animals, plants, famous people and so on.

COMMENT

An adaptable game which can be made easy or difficult by the clues given and the degree of difficulty of the answer words.

TALKING IT THROUGH

Verbal games

WORD ASSOCIATION

MATERIALS

None.

PREPARATION

None.

ACTION

Everyone sits in a circle. One participant starts by stating a subject such as 'water'. The player on his left repeats the word and then mentions something that is suggested to him by the word. This could be 'boats'. The person on his left repeats 'water' and 'boats' and adds something else suggested to him by 'boats', which might be 'the sea'. And so the game continues round the circle, each player repeating what has been previously said and adding another association of his own.

VARIATION

Simplify by not having to repeat the previous words. Each player states only what he associates with the word given by the player before him. It is important to have participants react and make their statements as quickly as possible without too much thought. See how long the association chain can be kept going without faltering and then begin again with a new word.

COMMENT

A useful memory exercise which is both stimulating and fun.

SUPERSTITIONS

MATERIALS

Pencils and paper.

PREPARATION

None.

ACTION

Each person writes down one superstition on a piece of paper. Examples:

Touch wood and avert an omen.

It is lucky to find a four-leaved clover.

It is unlucky to knock a chair over.

Salt protects you from bad luck.

Walking under a ladder brings bad luck.

Brides must wear something old, new, borrowed and blue.

The weather on a wedding day foretells the future of a marriage.

Now collect the pieces of paper and place them in the centre of the group. Ask for a volunteer to pick one and read it out. Then have a few minutes' discussion on the superstition and its possible origins, the truth or untruth of it, experiences regarding that particular superstition, and so on. After an allotted time, have a second player pick and read out another superstition. Continue in this fashion until everyone has read out.

VARIATIONS

Substitute proverbs or quotations for superstitions. Alternatively, have players write a statement on a piece of paper and then follow the same procedure.

COMMENT

Good for interaction. People love talking about superstitions and related experiences. To shorten the time taken to play the game and to make it easier, have the proverbs and so on written out beforehand. Players then choose one and read it out.

NEWS ITEM

MATERIALS

None.

PREPARATION

None.

ACTION

Form a circle. Explain that you want each player to cast his mind back over the events of the past week and to think about the nicest thing that has happened to him during that period. It may be something simple like receiving a letter from a friend, a phone call, a pleasant walk in the sunshine. It could be a birthday party, a shopping spree or anything at all. Allow a couple of minutes for thought, then ask players to take turns at sharing their news item with the others. Emphasise that you want the incident to be described in full, along with the pleasure it gave them.

VARIATIONS

1   Other openings which can be used are:
    a)   The funniest thing . . .
    b)   The worst thing . . .
    c)   The oddest thing . . .
    You will be able to think of more such openings.
2   Have players write their news items down on pieces of paper. Place these in a hat and have them drawn and read at random. See if participants can match the item to the correct person.

COMMENT

A particularly happy game which is uplifting. It is important to encourage participants to talk about the pleasant or funny side of the news item.

GEOGRAPHIC CIRCLE

MATERIALS

None.

PREPARATION

None.

ACTION

Have the participants sit in a circle. One player starts by calling out the name of a place. It may be a town, city, county or country and be anywhere in the world. For example, the first player could call out "London". The person next to him thinks of another place beginning with the last letter of the place previously stated — in this case the letter 'N'. He might say, "Nevada". The next player then says something else beginning with the letter 'A'. And so the game continues round the circle. No player can call out a place previously named. If, for example, the letter 'A' came up several times, each player would have to call out a different place. See how many times the game can be kept going round the circle.

VARIATIONS

Use other categories such as flowers, animals and so on.

COMMENT

If any player has difficulty, allow the others to help by giving clues but not actually stating the place to be named.

IMPROMPTU SPEECHES

MATERIALS

Paper, pencil and a bag.

PREPARATION

Write a number of subjects on pieces of paper and place them in a bag. Examples:

My career.

The cost of living.

Understanding the opposite sex.

A day by the sea.

Training a dog.

My favourite hobby.

School days.

How to stay healthy.

My favourite time of year.

ACTION

Seat the participants in a circle and have each take a piece of paper from the bag. Give a moment or two for thought and ask a volunteer to start by giving a one-minute talk on the subject selected. Encourage a light-hearted, amusing approach. When the first person has finished and been applauded, allow some time for discussion and comments on the talk. Afterwards another player is asked to give his impromptu speech.

VARIATION

Introduce the game as 'Nonsense speeches'. Players talk nonsense about the given topic for one minute. Write appropriate topics on the pieces of paper. Examples:

New uses for old bathtubs.

Teaching animals to talk.

The Mad Hatter was an alien from outer space.

A question which cannot be answered.

People who live underwater.

The Yo-Yo theory.

A tasteless invention.

The confessions of a fly.

Santa Claus is alive and well and living in a villa in Spain.

End the game by having a vote to find out who gave the most ridiculous or funniest talk.

COMMENT

Embarked on with a sense of fun, this exercise promotes good interaction and imaginative thinking.

BRIC-À-BRAC

MATERIALS

An assortment of toys, trinkets, postcards, mementoes, gifts and so on.

PREPARATION

None.

ACTION

Seat the group in a circle with the assortment of items in the centre. Ask participants to look at them for a moment or two and then pick up one item which brings back some memory. It could be a toy from their childhood, a holiday, a happy time, a sad time, an animal which was a pet and so on. Give a little time for thought and then request that each person in turn share that memory with the rest of the group.

VARIATION

Have participants invent a short incident or story around the item chosen.

COMMENT

This is a very pleasant exercise which helps participants get to know each other better, express feelings, trust each other with their thoughts and improve their self-confidence.

WORD CIRCLE

MATERIALS

A bean bag or soft ball.

PREPARATION

None.

ACTION

Arrange the participants in a circle with one player sitting in the centre. This person closes his eyes and the people seated in the circle pass the bean bag round the circle. It may go to left or right and change direction at any time. When he feels like it, the player in the centre calls out a letter of the alphabet. The person who has the bean bag at that moment must say ten words beginning with that letter within one minute. Plurals, proper names and places are not allowed. Other players may give clues to help but must not give actual words. If the player states ten words within the time, the person in the centre closes his eyes again and players begin to pass the bean bag again until another letter is called out. Should any player fail to state ten words within the time limit he changes places with the person in the centre of the circle.

VARIATIONS

Make the game more difficult by limiting the words to categories such as flowers, places, animals and so on. In these instances it will probably be necessary to reduce the number of words required to five and the time limit to thirty seconds. Even then, this variation is quite difficult.

COMMENT

To keep the game low-key and easy stipulate that the more difficult letters such as X, Z and Q are not used.

COUNTRYSIDE STORY

MATERIALS

None.

PREPARATION

None.

ACTION

Have the participants sit in a circle with one player standing in the centre. This person invents a story about the countryside. He may begin by describing the scene, the season and what is happening. It could be a story of adventure, a fantasy or a romance. At some point he must introduce an animal into the story. When he does so, everyone must change seats, moving at least three seats away. During the change-over, the person telling the story also tries to attain a seat in the circle. Whoever is left standing stays in the centre and goes on with the story until eventually another animal is introduced into the narrative. Everyone then changes seats again. And so the game continues.

VARIATIONS

Substitute flowers, birds, fish or particular words for animals.

COMMENT

A game which is fun and provokes imagination, quick thinking and the ability to speak in front of others.

SUSPENSION OF DISBELIEF

MATERIALS

None.

PREPARATION

None.

ACTION

Request that players select a partner. Instruct each individual to think of an invention which is beyond belief, the more ridiculous the better. It may be some sort of mechanical apparatus, a theory, a way of doing some day-to-day task, a new mode of travel and so on. After a few minutes for thought, one person tells his partner all about his invention without laughing. The partner must encourage the inventor by asking questions to find out all about the invention. After the first person has fully described his creation or an allotted time is up, have the partners change roles. The second player tells about his invention. Once more the listener helps the inventor by asking questions.

VARIATIONS

Instead of inventions, have the players think up incredible situations at work or a fantastic and unbelievable journey.

COMMENT

A game to help participants explore situations and ideas. It also aids listening and conversational skills.

MATERIALS

None.

PREPARATION

As each player arrives ask them for a personal item. This may be anything they choose: jewellery, a cigarette lighter, a pen, a scarf and so on. Do not allow the other participants to see what each individual gives you.

ACTION

Have everyone sit in a circle. Place the objects on a small table in the centre or on the floor so that they can be seen by everybody. Ask a player to pick up any item that is not his own and state to whom he thinks it belongs, why he thinks so and what sort of person would own such an object. If he is right about the owner that player must own up and correct any misleading statements which have been made. Proceed around the circle in this manner. When participants guess the owners wrongly, as they often will, allow them to make their statements before the named player denies ownership. Allow up to three wrong guesses before moving on to the next player. If the owner of the object has not given himself away at this stage you can either ask him to own up or continue with the game. Eventually someone will choose the item again and guess correctly.

VARIATIONS

Have participants select a partner. Ask each player to give his partner three items from about his person. These could be a tie, a shoe or a piece of jewellery. This time there is no need to conceal ownership. Allow a few minutes for thought, then ask each person to tell the rest of the group what he has learned about his partner from each of the three items. The owner of the objects corrects any errors.

COMMENT

People are always fascinated by what others have to say about them, which makes this a good game for interaction. It also necessitates the use of observation and is good fun.

AMBITIONS

MATERIALS

Pencils and paper.

PREPARATION

None.

ACTION

Have the group sit in a circle. Give out pencils and paper. Ask each person to write down a hope, aspiration or ambition for the future. Hopes might include going on holiday, visiting a friend, having a meal out, writing a letter, enrolling at evening class, moving house and so on. Have everyone fold their piece of paper and place it in a bag. Shake the bag and then ask for a volunteer to select one item and read it out. Everyone now tries to guess who wrote down the ambition. If a player picks his own out of the bag he must keep quiet about it until someone guesses. When the writer has been discovered, have a short discussion: how can the aspiration be achieved? Why does the person want to do it? And so on.

VARIATIONS

There are many variations on this theme. Following the same procedure, invite participants to write down:

a) likes and dislikes;
b) fears;
c) regrets;
d) an early memory;
e) a hobby enjoyed;
f) a happy memory;
g) a past achievement;
h) someone famous they'd like to meet.

COMMENT

Always popular, this exercise can be used for positive reinforcement or simply to allow people to share fears, experiences and so on.

TRUE INCIDENT

MATERIALS

None.

PREPARATION

None.

ACTION

Sit everyone in a circle. Explain that you want people to search their memories for significant moments in their lives: a memorable occasion, how they achieved something, a holiday they had, something they made and so on. Allow a few minutes for thought and then ask each person to relate his story to the group. Encourage the story-teller to elaborate, describing in detail and giving a full account. Have other players ask questions to help.

VARIATIONS

1 Instead of a true incident, have everyone make up a fictional story, the more outrageous and exaggerated the better. Let the theme be something they wished they had done, achieved or may want to do in the future.

2 Have the other players repeat each story, telling it from a different angle, so that the story may be seen from different viewpoints. If the story was about a holiday it might be seen from the courier's angle, an older or younger person's viewpoint, or through the eyes of the hotel receptionist.

COMMENT

A game which, when elaborated upon, can be very funny and stimulate the imagination. It is also pleasant to recall positive incidents from the past. Variation two above may help players to appreciate how their actions are viewed by others.

YES OR NO

MATERIALS

Coins or beads.

PREPARATION

None.

ACTION

Give each participant five beads. Players then pair off and engage each other in conversation. Partners should ask each other questions, the aim being to trick the other player into saying 'yes' or 'no'. Any person who answers a question with 'yes' or 'no' is given a bead by the questioner, after which the two players split up and move on to choose new partners. The first person to get rid of his five beads is the winner.

VARIATIONS

A more simple version of this game is sometimes known as 'odds and evens'. Each player is given ten beads. He may put any number of them in one clenched hand, choose an opponent and ask: "Odds or evens?" If the opponent guesses wrongly he is given a bead. If the guess is correct he gives a bead to the questioner. The players then split up and seek new opponents. The first player to get rid of all his beads is the winner.

COMMENT

A game which is good fun and enables players to learn about each other. Also it stimulates quick thinking.

MATERIALS

None — but a pile of old jumble for use as props and for dressing up may add authenticity.

PREPARATION

Invent some basic situations such as:

1 A person walking home comes upon some neighbours arguing and tries to intervene.
2 A couple return from holiday to find someone else living in their house.
3 A group of people are in an aeroplane when a fire breaks out.
4 A man is in a restaurant with his wife when a strange girl comes over, kisses him and joins them at the table — then states that she, too, is married to him.
5 A couple arrive at a previously booked hotel to find that there has been an error and they cannot have a room. Everywhere else is also fully booked.

ACTION

Split the participants into three or four small groups. Give each group a different situation and ask them to develop it, having two or three things happening in sequence. In situation (1) above, the person going home could be drawn into an argument. The police turn up, having been told of a disturbance. The person could be accused by the others of being the cause and be taken away by the police. At the police station the person is very upset until someone turns up and explains, for example, that there had been a misinterpretation of what was going on. All the players have to improvise their own dialogue and each person should have a part in the sketch. It is often a good idea to have a narrator to introduce the scene and explain the changes of surroundings from street to police station and so on.

Give the groups ten or fifteen minutes to work out what they are going to do and then have them perform in turn for the other groups. Make sure that each sketch is applauded. Afterwards discuss how it felt to do the performance and what people feel are the benefits of activities like this.

VARIATION

Give each group three objects in a bag and ask them to invent a short sketch in which all the items are used or connected logically.

COMMENT

There is plenty of scope provided here for imaginative thinking. People are usually much more creative than they think they are. An excellent exercise for building confidence, developing the ability to speak in front of others, interaction and teamwork.

MATERIALS

None.

PREPARATION

None.

ACTION

Have the participants form a circle. One player calls out a number such as 'Seven'. The person on his left then calls out an association with the number. He could say: "Seven deadly sins!" Then he adds another number, which might be 'Sixteen'. The person on his left could say: "Sweet sixteen!" The game continues in this manner. If the player answering thinks there is no association with the number he may challenge the person who called it out. If that person cannot state an association he is eliminated, as is anyone unable to provide an association. The procedure continues until only one player is left and declared the winner.

VARIATION

Have players each call out a number in turn. As each person does so, anyone in the remainder of the group can state an association with the number.

COMMENT

If you do not wish to eliminate players, have a points system: one point for every successful association and a point against players who are successfully challenged.

WHAT ARE YOU WEARING?

MATERIALS

None.

PREPARATION

None.

ACTION

Have the players choose a partner, one with whom they feel comfortable. Give them a couple of minutes to shake hands, introduce themselves and decide who is to be A and who B. Now announce that A is going to tell B the story of what he, A, is wearing and, at the same time, B will help his partner by asking questions about each item until all clothes and jewellery have been explained. A might begin: "I bought this scarf at a jumble sale. The blouse — I searched weeks before I found the right colour but eventually I came across this gem in the summer sale", and so on. B's typical questions might be: "What a pretty necklace! Was it a present? Is that your engagement ring?", and so on. It is important that player B helps player A in this manner. Allow about three or four minutes and then ask B to give an account of what he is wearing. This time, player A asks the questions.

VARIATION

Divide the players into small groups of three, four or five people. Have one player telling the story and the others helping him by asking questions.

COMMENT

A self-awareness game that is also a good ice-breaker.

MATERIALS

Cassette recorder and cassette, or record-player and records.

PREPARATION

Write out a list of topics. Examples:

1   Royalty.
2   Likes and dislikes.
3   The last film, play or television show you saw.
4   Your favourite food.
5   Modern music.
6   Your favourite pastime.
7   Should caning in schools be made compulsory?
8   A woman's place is in the home.
9   Moral values today.
10 What would you do with the money if you won in a lottery?

ACTION

Have the group form two circles — an inner and outer ring — comprising the same number of players. Explain that you are going to play some music and that, while it is playing, you want the inner circle to move round to the left and the outer circle to move to the right. When the music stops everyone stands still facing a partner. A topic is announced from the prepared list. Each person now introduces himself by name to his partner, expresses his views on the subject and they proceed to discuss it. When the music restarts — after about two or three minutes — everyone begins to circle again until the music stops once more and another topic is announced. The game continues in this manner.

VARIATION

Instead of forming circles have people walking freely around the room. Each time the music stops the players must find a new partner.

COMMENT

Make sure that the list of topics is one which will appeal to the group, bearing in mind age, interests and so on. It is a good idea to include topical items, both local and national. A game to encourage discussion and interaction.

EMERGENCY

MATERIALS

None.

PREPARATION

None.

ACTION

Instruct one player to leave the room. While he is out he must think of a question beginning: 'What would happen if you . . .?', and add an emergency situation. Examples: What would happen if you —

broke a leg?

had a nosebleed?

got lost at sea?

found a thousand pounds?

The people remaining in the room each think of a solution to a mishap, accident or adventure. After a few moments players whisper their solutions to the person on their left. Then the player outside is invited back into the room. He asks everyone in turn: "What would happen if you . . .?" (adding the situation he has dreamed up). Each player answers with the solution he has been given by his neighbour. When everyone has had a turn at answering, another person can be asked to leave the room and think up a new emergency question.

COMMENT

A delightful activity which provides a lot of fun.

PICTURE STORY

MATERIALS

Pictures and scissors.

PREPARATION

Obtain pictures from magazines or a similar source and cut them in two — jigsaw fashion. If you have ten players in the group, you will need five pictures — half a picture for each person.

ACTION

Give out the half-pictures at random, making sure that they are well jumbled. Ask each player to find the person with the other half of his picture. Request that partners sit together, chat for a few minutes and invent a story about the picture. This may be a fictional fantasy, a real-life story from memory sparked off by the picture, or a description of the picture and what the players feel about it. Allow freedom of choice or, alternatively, get people to stick to a theme. When an allotted time is up, have the players sit in a circle and partners share telling each story to the group.

VARIATIONS

The pictures may be cut up into three or four pieces, with small groups being formed. Each group can then elect a spokesman to relate the story. Alternatively, allow each player in the group to tell part of the story.

COMMENT

When kept simple, this game is a pleasant activity for players who are not very familiar with each other. To make it more fun, players can be asked to invent an amusing story about the picture. You would, of course, bear any theme in mind when choosing the pictures.

THE TRAVELLER'S ALPHABET

MATERIALS

None.

PREPARATION

None.

ACTION

The participants sit in a circle. One player turns to the person on his left and asks: "Where are you going?" The person answering states the name of a country, city or town beginning with the letter 'A'. The first player then asks: "What will you do there?" The second person answers describing an activity, using a verb, an adjective and a noun, all beginning with the letter 'A'. For example:

First player	"Where are you going?"
Second player	"Austria."
First player	"What will you do there?"
Second player	"Arrange active activities."

The second player now goes through the same procedure with a third person. This time the player answers with words beginning with the letter 'B'. For example:

Second player	"Where are you going?"
Third player	"Birmingham."
Second player	"What will you do there?"
Third player	"Build big bikes."

The game continues in the same manner round the circle, going through the alphabet.

VARIATION

Play as a team game with a spokesman for one team putting the questions to another team. Have a time limit of one minute for the answers, with points for correct answers and penalty points for failure to beat the clock.

COMMENT

A game for quick and imaginative thinking.

WRITE IT DOWN
Pen and paper games

WRITE A LETTER

MATERIALS

Pencils and paper.

PREPARATION

None.

ACTION

Hand out pencils and paper and then ask each player to write a letter of the alphabet at the top of the paper. It can be any letter at all. Do, however, warn against difficult letters such as Q, W, X and Z. Instruct each person to construct a letter in which every word used begins with the letter of the alphabet he has written on the top of his sheet of paper. Allow about ten minutes and then ask each person to read out what he has written. The player who has written the longest or the most amusing letter can be announced the winner.

VARIATIONS

Instead of a letter, have players write a news item, biography or incident following the same procedure.

COMMENT

This is quite difficult, especially if too serious an attitude is adopted. Encourage a light-hearted, amusing approach.

CHARACTER TRAITS

MATERIALS

Pencils, paper and a small bag.

PREPARATION

None.

ACTION

Seat the players in a circle and give out pencils and paper. Ask each player to write down one trait which is characteristic of himself. If desirable, request that it be a positive trait. Examples:

enthusiastic	modest	quiet
energetic	affectionate	jolly
talkative	sullen	gentle
optimistic	shy	vain

If necessary, before asking players to write, have them call out traits at random and write a long list on the blackboard.

When players have finished writing the characteristic have them fold their pieces of paper and place them in a bag. Give the bag a good shake, pass it round the circle and have each player take out a paper. If, by chance, someone chooses his own he must not say so but continue as if it is someone else's. Now ask a volunteer to read out from the chosen piece of paper. All the other players try to guess who wrote it. They will often choose wrongly, giving opportunity for discussion and a chance for the players to gain some idea of how others see them.

VARIATIONS

1 Players write one positive and one negative trait about themselves.
2 Ask one group member to leave the room, then ask people to write something positive about the absent person. Mix up the papers. When the player is called back into the room he tries to guess who wrote what.

144

COMMENT

This activity is good for positive reinforcement, confidence-building and increasing self-awareness.

ALL WAYS

MATERIALS

Blackboard and chalk or a large sheet of paper and a magic marker.

PREPARATION

None.

ACTION

One player is asked to write a word in the centre of the blackboard. This can be any word he pleases. The next player is asked to add another word, building in any way he chooses from the first word, as in *Figure 7.1*. A third player adds another word and so the procedure continues, building as far as possible from the basic word. Letters which fall adjacent to each other must also make a word.

Figure 7.1

VARIATION

Hand each player a sheet of paper and pencil. Give a word to be written in the centre of the page. Now see who can write out the most words in an allotted time.

COMMENT

An enjoyable game which is easy to play.

ELEPHANTS

MATERIALS

Large sheets of drawing paper and magic markers, pens or pencils.

PREPARATION

None.

ACTION

Divide the players into teams of about five people. Pin as many sheets of drawing paper on the wall as there are teams. Alternatively, have each team gather round a table. Ask each team to number its members one to five and then instruct that number: one, draws the head; two, the legs and feet; three, the tail; four, the body; five, the trunk. Having made sure that each person knows which part of the elephant he has to draw, call out the numbers in any order. The trunk could be drawn first, the tail second, the legs and feet third and so on. When each elephant is complete have all the members vote to see which is best.

VARIATIONS

Use other animals as the subject, such as camels, tigers or horses. Also use birds and reptiles.

COMMENT

A simple activity, but one which provides a lot of fun and enjoyment.

SELF-ADVERT

MATERIALS

Pencils, paper and a box.

PREPARATION

None.

ACTION

Give each player a pencil and some paper. Ask each member of the group to write an advert recommending himself as a friend. No more than thirty words can be used and all his best points should be highlighted. When this has been completed collect the pieces of paper and place them in a box. Give them a good shuffle and hand out at random or have players dip into the box and select one for themselves. Explain that if any participant has picked his own advert he must remain silent about this and pretend it is someone else's. Ask players in turn to read out the advert now in their possession. Players try to guess who has written the advert.

VARIATIONS

1   A variety of topics can be chosen for this game. For example, have participants write adverts recommending themselves as:

   a) a sweetheart;   e) an employee;

   b) a partner;   f) a companion;

   c) a brother or a sister; g) a landlord;

   d) an employer;   h) a tenant.

   Many more ideas will occur to you.

2   Ask players to write adverts recommending another member of the group as a friend or any of the above. The group can attempt to guess both the author and about whom it has been written.

COMMENT

An excellent game for positive reinforcement. It is also a lot of fun, especially when players are encouraged to exaggerate their attributes.

RANDOM WORDS

MATERIALS

Pencils and paper.

PREPARATION

None.

ACTION

Ask participants to call out ten words at random and write them on a blackboard. Request that each person construct a paragraph — of 50 to 100 words — which includes the ten words written on the blackboard, presented as naturally as possible. Allow fifteen to twenty minutes and then have each person read out his paragraph. Invite comments after each reading and, if possible, vote to elect the best and most ingenious paragraph.

VARIATIONS

When choosing the random words, select ten words associated with a category. For example, here are ten words which could be associated with 'youth':

juvenile	prime	lazy
irresponsible	teenage	school
immature	careless	
studious	adolescent	

Other categories:

old age	travel	happiness
success	love	friendship

COMMENT

Many more categories can be added to the above.

COAT OF ARMS

MATERIALS

Pencils, paper and a small box.

PREPARATION

Think of six topics for a coat of arms. Here is an example, using 'the family' as a theme.

1 What single word most aptly describes your family?
2 Which aspect of life causes most controversy within your family?
3 What saying or catch-phrase is often used in your family?
4 What is your family fantasy?
5 Make up a family motto.
6 What epitaph do you think would be appropriate for your family?

ACTION

Give each player a pencil and some paper. Ask them to draw a shield outline as shown in *Figure 7.2*. The drawing should be about six

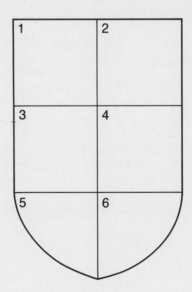

Figure 7.2

inches high and four inches wide. Read out the first topic on your list and allow a few minutes for everyone to write their contribution in one of the sections. Continue in the same manner until all six sections have something written in them. Collect all the shields and place them in a box. Make sure they are jumbled. Have players pick a shield out of the box, one at a time, and read out what is written on it. All participants try to guess whose shield has been read out. When the player has been found out, have a short discussion on what he has written.

VARIATIONS

1 Allow the players to choose their own themes and topics.
2 Simplify the game by preparing the drawings and having them ready to hand out to the players; use only three topics. This is easily accommodated, by leaving out the vertical line on the shield.

COMMENT

This is another game which can be kept simple or made more demanding. To keep on an amusing level, choose humorous topics or instruct the players to exaggerate and use their imaginations in an amusing way. When used on a more serious level, choose the topics accordingly and introduce appropriately, acknowledging what can be expected from the participants.

TELEGRAMS

MATERIALS

Pencils and paper.

PREPARATION

None.

ACTION

Give all the players a pencil and a sheet of paper. Ask them to write down the same word at the top of the page. This can be any word you please. Examples: birthday, abstraction, dissatisfaction, perpendicular, partner and so on. Next, ask each person to write a telegram to a friend. Each word of the telegram must start with one of the letters of the word given and be in the same order.

Example   ABSTRACTION
Telegram   Arrived Berlin. Sold the radio. Actually completed the itinerary. Oscar non-committal.

After a pre-set time, or when everyone has completed the telegrams, have each person read out what he has written.

VARIATION

Ask each member of the group to call out a letter of the alphabet. Exclude the use of Q, X and Z. Players write down the letters as they are called out, keeping them in the same order. Now each person writes a telegram using all the letters.

COMMENT

A good exercise to inspire imaginative thinking and one which provides lots of laughter and interaction.

CONSEQUENCES

MATERIALS

Pencils and paper.

PREPARATION

Write out a list of instructions for the stories.

ACTION

Each player is given a long slip of paper and a pencil. The object is to write as many stories as there are players, with as many players as possible contributing a part of each story. Start by giving instructions for the first part of the story. This is usually: 'Write a person's name'. Players write down a name. The sheet of paper is folded over to hide what has been written and then passed on to the neighbour on each player's left. Instructions for the next part of the story are given and players write it without looking at what has previously been written. The procedure is repeated until the story is completed. A very short story might have these writing instructions:

1   A man's name.
2   The word 'met', followed by a woman's name.
3   The place where they met.
4   What he said.
5   What she said.
6   And the consequence was . . .

When the stories are finished, the folded papers are passed on for the last time and, one by one, players unfold them and read out each story.

VARIATIONS

Vary the instructions to suit the group. A longer story might have these instructions:

1   A word which describes someone's appearance.
2   A girl's name.
3   The word 'met' and a description of a man's character.
4   A man's name.
5   Where the two people met.

6   What the circumstances were.
7   When they met.
8   What he said to her.
9   What she said to him.
10 What he did.
11 What she did.
12 What the consequence was . . .
13 And what the neighbours said.

COMMENT

A game guaranteed to provide a lot of fun.

ADVICE

MATERIALS

Pencils and paper.

PREPARATION

None.

ACTION

Arrange the players in a circle and give them each a pencil and a sheet of paper. Ask them to write a sentence or two giving a piece of advice to someone else. It may be something they have learned from their own experience. The advice need not be to anyone in the group, but can be to an imaginary person or a friend, son, mother and so on.

When everyone has finished writing, collect the pieces of paper and mix them up. Invite players to select a piece of paper and read out the advice. Discuss the advice, the wisdom of it and the circumstances in which it might hold true. Who would not take the advice and why? After the discussion, if the person who wrote it wants to own up give an opportunity to do so. The game continues until each player has read out a piece of advice.

COMMENT

There is no need for all the advice to be of a serious or profound nature. Encourage a good-humoured approach. An excellent exercise for encouraging interaction and aiding expression.

JUMBLED CITIES

MATERIALS

Pencils and paper.

PREPARATION

Write out a list of cities and jumble up the letters. Examples:

Cape Town	AEPC WNTO
Lisbon	NOSBIL
Madrid	IRDDAM
Vienna	NVEIAN
Prague	UPARGE
London	NNOOLD

ACTION

Either write the jumbled city list on the blackboard or hand out a photocopied list with a space for the participants to write in the city. Give an allotted time for players to complete the list. When the time is up, have players call out the answers.

VARIATIONS

Many variations are possible. For example, use jumbled countries, plants, animals, birds, fish, rivers, politicians, authors, books, films, film stars and so on.

COMMENT

While some time is needed to prepare these lists, once prepared they can be kept and used repeatedly. A good idea is to split participants into two teams and have each team prepare their own list to challenge the other. Give one team cities and the other countries, or whatever you like. Once the lists are complete, note them down and have them typed and copied.

CLUMPS

MATERIALS

Sheets of drawing paper and magic markers or pencils.

PREPARATION

Draw up a list of occupations. Here are a few:

bus driver	nurse	typist
carpenter	chef	painter
car salesman	librarian	gardener
policeman	housewife	fireman
doctor	steeplejack	musician
hairdresser	singer	dentist
dancer	postman	telephone operator

ACTION

Divide the group into teams. Give each team a large sheet of drawing paper and something to draw with. One member from each team approaches the group leader who whispers one of the occupations so that the team members cannot hear, or, alternatively, writes down the word and shows it to him. Individuals return to their teams and draw an illustration to represent the occupation. The illustrator must not speak except to say 'no' or 'yes'. The other team members try to guess the occupation. When they do, another team member approaches the group leader to be told another job. And so the game continues. The first team to guess all the occupations is the winner.

VARIATIONS

Also use lists of objects, nursery rhymes, fairy-tales and activities such as moving house, playing football, flying a kite and so on.

COMMENT

This activity stimulates thinking, prompts imagination, encourages interaction and is good fun.

PERSONAL STATEMENTS

MATERIALS

Pencils, paper and a bag.

PREPARATION

None.

ACTION

Seat the players in a circle and give each person a pencil and paper. Ask them to write five personal statements, each one beginning with: 'I am . . .' A typical example:

I am ambitious.

I am very stubborn.

I am lacking in confidence.

I am unable to resist eating doughnuts.

I am very loyal.

Now have them fold their papers and place them in a bag. Shake the bag and ask for a volunteer to select one and read it out. Players have to guess the author and hold a two-minute discussion on what has been written. Then another paper is taken from the bag. The game continues in this manner until all the statements have been read out.

VARIATIONS

There are many alternatives. Here are a few more beginnings which can be used:

1   My ambition is . . .
2   I believe . . .
3   I am good at . . .
4   I fear . . .
5   I am going to . . .

COMMENT

A self-awareness exercise which also stimulates interaction and can be used for positive reinforcement.

PERSONAL STATEMENTS

MATERIALS

Pencils, paper and a bag.

PREPARATION

None.

ACTION

Seat the players in a circle and give each person a pencil and paper. Ask them to write five personal statements, each one beginning with: 'I am . . .' A typical example:

I am ambitious.

I am very stubborn.

I am lacking in confidence.

I am unable to resist eating doughnuts.

I am very loyal.

Now have them fold their papers and place them in a bag. Shake the bag and ask for a volunteer to select one and read it out. Players have to guess the author and hold a two-minute discussion on what has been written. Then another paper is taken from the bag. The game continues in this manner until all the statements have been read out.

VARIATIONS

There are many alternatives. Here are a few more beginnings which can be used:

1 My ambition is . . .
2 I believe . . .
3 I am good at . . .
4 I fear . . .
5 I am going to . . .

COMMENT

A self-awareness exercise which also stimulates interaction and can be used for positive reinforcement.

USE YOUR KNOWLEDGE

General and impromptu quizzes

NEWSPAPER QUIZ

MATERIALS

Several copies of the same daily newspaper, pencils and paper.

PREPARATION

Read through the paper, including the advertisements, and write out at least ten questions concerning the contents.

ACTION

Hand out a copy of the same newspaper to each player. Allow about ten minutes for them to read through it and then collect the papers. Now hand out pencils and paper and ask your questions. Have everyone write the answers or, if you wish, the game can be played verbally. As appropriate, discuss the answers and what is happening in the news. Points can be given for correct answers.

VARIATIONS

1   Use as a team game with teams composing the questions for their opponents, or have each player put one question to the other players.
2   Use current magazines or colour supplements instead of newspapers.

COMMENT

A good game for making participants aware of what is currently happening in the world.

MATERIALS

Dictionaries equal to the number of teams to be formed, pencils and paper.

PREPARATION

None.

ACTION

Split the players into two or more teams. Give each team a dictionary and instruct them to make a list of about twenty words with the letter E in them. When the list is complete, have them re-write it leaving out the letter E in each word. Here are some examples:

Obese — OBS	Eager — AGR	Bevel — BVL
News — NWS	Genre — GNR	Eagle — AGL
Isle — ISL	Eaten — ATN	Erect — RCT
Blue — BLU	Lever — LVR	Fete — FT

Next, have each team take turns at challenging the other teams by calling out their list of 'words' without Es. The first team to call out the correct word each time wins a point. If no one gets it then the challenging team is awarded a point. The team with the most points at the end of the game wins.

VARIATIONS

Omit other letters of the alphabet, preferably vowels, from words.

COMMENT

To allow for teams presenting the same word, have each team list a few extra words to be held in reserve. Each team can also be given a different letter to omit. However, bear in mind that E is the most common letter used and that other letters, such as Q, X, Y and Z, present difficulties.

GUESS THE OBJECT

MATERIALS

None.

PREPARATION

None.

ACTION

Seat the players in a circle and ask for a volunteer to leave the room. While he is out, the remaining players think of an object. This can be anything: a bed, a car, a potato, a fish, the moon, a book, and so on. Once an object has been decided upon, call the volunteer back into the room. This player, by asking each person in the circle a question, tries to guess the object. Typical questions might be:

"Is it edible?"

"Is it manufactured?"

"Is it blue?"

"Have you got one?"

"Do you use it first thing in the morning?"

The person answering must use only 'yes' or 'no'. The questions continue until the object is discovered.

VARIATIONS

1 Conversely, have one player think of an object and all the other players ask the questions to enable them to guess the word.
2 Instead of objects, use adjectives. Have players guess words such as handsome, ugly, sad, angry, sleek, flat, honest.

COMMENT

A game which encourages participation, provokes quick thinking and helps to build confidence.

HOW OBSERVANT ARE YOU?

MATERIALS

A large book: this can be a biography, a history book or a novel. Pencils and paper.

PREPARATION

Write out a list of questions about the book. Examples:

1 What was the title?
2 Who was the author?
3 Who was the publisher?
4 How many pages were there in the book?
5 Was there a dedication?
6 What colour was the cover?
7 Did the book contain illustrations?
8 Was there an introduction?
9 Were the pages numbered at the top or the bottom?
10 How many chapters did the book contain?

Many other questions can be added. The player gets only a glance at the book, so do not ask questions which demand a detailed reading for answers.

ACTION

Seat the players in a circle. Pass the book around the players, giving each person about one minute to examine it. When everyone has had a good look, put the book away somewhere it cannot be seen. Give everyone a pencil and some paper and ask them to write down the answer to each question on your list. The person with the most correct is the winner.

VARIATIONS

Follow the same procedure for other types of objects such as an empty biscuit tin or a picture containing lots of detail.

COMMENT

A good observation and memory game.

INITIAL PROVERBS

MATERIALS

Pencils, paper and a book of proverbs.

PREPARATION

Make a list of proverbs. List them again on a separate sheet, this time writing down only the intitial letter in each word. Examples:

L___ b_____ y__ L__ (Look before you leap)

E____ d__ h__ h__ d__ (Every dog has his day)

O__ o_ s____, o__ o_ m___ (Out of sight, out of mind)

P____ g___ b_____ a f___ (Pride goes before a fall)

Have this sheet photocopied.

ACTION

Hand out the photocopies and allow a set time for the players to fill in the answers. When these are completed, have players call out their answers and discuss the truth or falsity of the proverbs. The person with the most correct is the winner.

VARIATION

Divide the group into two teams. Have each team make up their own initial proverb list and then challenge each other.

COMMENT

A game in which everyone can participate and which provides good opportunity for interaction.

NOVELTY NOUGHTS-AND-CROSSES

MATERIALS

Paper, glue, a magic marker and a quiz book.

PREPARATION

Using paper strips, make up arm bands for two teams — one half with
Os and the other half with Xs written boldly on them. Also set out
empty chairs in three rows of three to represent a noughts and
crosses grid. Either compile some general knowledge questions or
use a quiz book.

ACTION

Divide the players into two teams. Give one team the O armbands
and the other the Xs. Teams take it in turn to answer a question. If a
team answers correctly, one member from the team sits on a chair in
the grid. If they fail to answer the question the team misses a turn and
the other team is asked the next question. Players seated in the grid
are not allowed to answer the questions. The first team to complete a
row of Os or Xs wins that particular game. Make it the best of five
games, or set a time limit.

VARIATIONS

1   Have individuals from each team answer questions and decide
    where to sit without advice from team mates.
2   Simplify the game; play noughts-and-crosses in this fashion but
    omit asking questions.
3   Draw a grid on a blackboard, then, on answering a question, each
    team can place an O or an X on the grid. To make the game more
    complicated subjects such as history, geography, famous people
    and so on can be placed at the top of each square in the grid.
    Teams must then answer questions on the subject to be able to
    place their O or X in each square.

COMMENT

A game which encourages players to think, make decisions, use their
memories and interact.

176

WORD POWER

MATERIALS

Pencils and paper.

PREPARATION

None.

ACTION

Divide the group into two or more teams. Instruct them to choose particular words and then write their meanings alongside — about fifteen or twenty should be sufficient. Examples:

1   Curling — A game in which heavy stones are slid towards a goal.
2   Infatuation — An unreasoning passion or a foolish love.
3   Koran — Moslem's sacred book.
4   Palmistry — Fortune-telling from the lines of the hand.
5   Marathon — A foot race of twenty-six miles.
6   Operetta — A musical play in a light vein.
7   Demonstrate — Show how to do something.
8   Trousseau — A bride's outfit.

When the lists have been completed the teams take turns at calling out just the meaning. The first opposing team to match the correct word to the meaning wins a point. The game continues until all the words from each team have been guessed.

COMMENT

Keep a dictionary to hand to check the meaning of words. If necessary, to make the game easier, give each team a dictionary at the outset of the game to assist in compiling the lists. The dictionaries must, of course, be reclaimed before teams call out the meanings.

WHO ARE THEY?

MATERIALS

Slips of paper and a small bag.

PREPARATION

Make a list of nicknames of famous people, together with their real names. Examples:

The Brat	John McEnroe
The Bitch	Joan Collins
The Duke	John Wayne
The Desert Fox	Field Marshal Rommel
The Iron Duke	The First Duke of Wellington
G.B.S.	George Bernard Shaw
Honest Abe	Abraham Lincoln
Winnie	Winston Churchill
Dizzy	Benjamin Disraeli
The Little Corporal	Napoleon
Monty	First Viscount Montgomery
Lord Haw Haw	William Joyce

Now write out only the nicknames again on slips of paper and place them in a bag.

ACTION

Divide the group into two teams. A member from one team selects a nickname from the bag and reads it out to his team who must answer with the real name within thirty seconds. Then a player from the opposing team chooses one and reads it out to his own team. Thus the game continues, with teams being awarded points for correct answers. Whichever team accumulates the most points is the winner.

VARIATIONS

Similar quizzes can be made up for:
1   Films and film stars.
2   Books and authors.

3 Songs and singers.

4 Fictitious characters from books and films.

COMMENT

This is always popular, and is yet another game which can be kept and used many times. The game can also be played with teams making up their own lists and challenging each other.

TELEVISION EXPERT

MATERIALS

None.

PREPARATION

None.

ACTION

Everyone is seated in a circle. One player stands in the centre of the group and states: "I am going to watch . . . [naming a personality and television programme] on the television." The player, having made his statement, then begins to ask each group member one question about the programme or personality. Examples:

"Is it a comedy?"

"To whom is the main character married?"

"What time is it on?"

"Which channel is it on?"

"What colour is the main character's hair?"

Each person who answers correctly is awarded a point. When the player asking the questions has put a question to everyone he sits down and another player has a turn. And so the game continues, until each person has had an opportunity to ask the questions. The player who has accumulated the most points can be declared 'television expert' of the day.

VARIATIONS

Follow the same procedure for:
1   Films and film stars.
2   Books and authors.
3   Famous people and places associated with them.

COMMENT

An activity which is fun, prompts quick thinking and builds confidence and the ability to converse within groups.

MATERIALS

Pencils and paper.

PREPARATION

Make a list of famous people who are likely to be well known to the participants.

ACTION

Give the players pencils and paper, then read out the surname of the first person on your list. The players write down the forename if they know it. If people do not remember the name but think they know the initials, they can put those down. When all the surnames have been called out, start at the beginning again and have the players call out the forenames. Players award themselves two points for full forenames and one point for initials. See who can accumulate the most points.

VARIATIONS

1   Write a list of forenames and surnames of famous people on a blackboard in a jumbled fashion. Players must try to match forenames and surnames correctly.
2   Write a list of films and film stars. Players match the film stars to the films in which they starred.
3   Write a list of authors and book titles. Players match the authors' names to their books.
4   Write a list of composers and musical scores. Players match the correct composers to scores.

COMMENT

Play any of the variations as a team quiz with teams preparing their own lists and challenging each other.

ALPHABET CARDS

MATERIALS

Card and a magic marker.

PREPARATION

Make up a pack of cards, marking one letter of the alphabet on each card with a magic marker. Omit the more difficult letters such as X, Y and Z. Also have some categories in mind, like places, flowers, animals, food, authors, cars and so on.

ACTION

Write the names of the chosen categories on a blackboard or large sheet of paper so that they are visible to all the players. Divide the group into two or more teams. Draw a card from the pack of alphabet cards and call out the letter written on it, along with the name of a category. The first player to call out the name of a place — if that is the category — wins a point for his team. Shuffle the cards, choose another and read out the letter, along with a different category. And so the game continues. The team which accumulates the most points is the winner.

VARIATION

Ask one team for a category of their own, then pick an alphabet card specifically for that team. The opposing team then chooses another category to their own liking and a card is drawn for them. Impose a time limit for the reply with penalty points awarded against those who fail to beat the clock.

COMMENT

This is a quiz requiring quick thinking and one in which most people can take part, so long as care is taken in selecting the categories. It can, of course, be made more demanding by choosing difficult categories.

THE GEOGRAPHY GAME

MATERIALS

None.

PREPARATION

None.

ACTION

Split the group into two teams. One team thinks of a town or city with the same number of letters as there are players in the team. If there are six players they might select 'Dallas'. One letter of the city is assigned to each person in the team who secretly thinks of another town or city beginning with his letter. In the example — Dallas — the player assigned with the letter D might select Dublin, the person assigned with A could choose Algiers, and so on. When this procedure has been completed the opposing team asks questions of each player in turn in order to ascertain their town. Examples:

"Is it in this country?"

"Is it in Europe?"

"Has it a hot climate?"

The questions are answered with 'Yes' or 'No' only. This continues until the opposing team has guessed all the towns or cities and can decipher all the beginning letters, the object being to discover the original city: Dallas. A time limit can be put on the questioning, with a penalty awarded against teams for not getting the answer within that time limit. Award points for success. The team which achieves the highest score over a series of games is the winner.

VARIATION

In order to make the game easier, the opposing team can ask each person to give a clue to the town or city he represents rather than have a questioning process.

COMMENT

A game which educates as well as encouraging interaction and stimulating quick thinking.

TOWNS AND COUNTIES

MATERIALS

None, but a gazetteer may come in handy.

PREPARATION

None.

ACTION

Divide the players into two teams, A and B. Team A confer amongst themselves and decide on the name of a town and the county in which it is situated. A spokesman for the team then calls out the name of the town and team B must state the county. If they can do so, they win a point; if not, team A is awarded a point. Team B then confers, decides upon a town and county and calls out the name of the town. Team A must state the county. And so the game continues.

VARIATIONS

1 Have teams call out a county and the other team must name a town within its boundaries.
2 Follow the same procedure for cities and countries.

COMMENT

To make the game easier, give each team a map or a gazetteer and have them prepare lists before challenging each other. In any case it is advisable to have a gazetteer handy to check any answers which may be queried.

GEOGRAPHY JIGSAW

MATERIALS

Card, a map of Europe and a magic marker.

PREPARATION

Using a map of Europe as a guide, draw or trace two outlines onto card, marking the borders of each country and labelling them. Now, cut out each country so that you have two sets of cards. More sets can be made if required.

ACTION

Divide the players into two or more teams. Jumble each set of country cards and give one set to each team. See who can put the cards together in the correct order. When an allotted time is up, have the teams call out the correct positions.

VARIATION

Trace or draw a map of any continent. Cut the map into countries and have teams put them together in the correct order. Alternatively, do the same for countries, dividing the map into states or counties.

COMMENT

A game that is fun, educational, promotes thinking, encourages sharing of knowledge and exercises memory.

THE MEMORY GAME

MATERIALS

Pencils and paper.

PREPARATION

Prepare a list of questions from a magazine feature article which is to be read out. Choose an item which contains a number of facts and details.

ACTION

Make sure that the players are seated so that they can hear your voice clearly and then read out the chosen article. Give a pencil and some paper to each player and begin asking the previously prepared questions. Give plenty of time for the participants to write down the answers. When all the questions have been asked, go back to the beginning again and have players shout out the answers. The person with the most correct wins. End the game by discussing how various players memorise things.

VARIATIONS

As well as feature articles use very short stories and news items.

COMMENT

A good memory game.

JACKPOT QUIZ

MATERIALS

A prize and a quiz book.

PREPARATION

Compile a list of simple general knowledge questions or obtain a quiz book.

ACTION

Using a compiled list or a quiz book, ask each player three questions. Each person who answers all his questions correctly goes forward to the next round. This time put two, slightly more difficult, questions to each person. Again, those who answer correctly go forward to a final round, when one even more difficult question is put to all the remaining players at the same time. The person who answers first wins the 'Jackpot' prize. More rounds can be added to the quiz simply by starting with four or five questions being put to each player.

VARIATION

Have rounds in which one question is put to each competitor; give a point for each correctly answered question. The person who accumulates the most points wins the 'Jackpot'.

COMMENT

The anticipation of a prize — no matter how small — always gives zest to the competition.

BOTTICELLI

MATERIALS

None.

PREPARATION

None.

ACTION

Seat the players in a circle. Ask one participant to think of a well-known person or fictitious character. He states the initial letter of the person's surname. The other players now endeavour to discover the name he has in mind by asking questions. If the participant had thought of George Bernard Shaw, another player may ask: "Are you a singer?" The questioned player must answer indirectly: "No, I am not Frank Sinatra." Having answered he must not be questioned further by that particular person. If he cannot think of a singer beginning with the letter S he can be asked a second question by the same questioner. This could be: "Are you dead?" He must now answer directly and truthfully, with "Yes" or "No".

Another player then asks his first question. This procedure continues until every player has had a chance to ask questions. If the group has not guessed the famous person, the player has won the round. Another participant then takes a turn at thinking of the name of a famous person. Competitors should aim to ask awkward questions so that they can proceed to ask another which must be answered in a direct manner with "Yes" or "No".

COMMENT

Concentration and quick thinking are needed for this game.

MUSICAL QUIZ

MATERIALS

Tape recorder, record-player, pencils and paper.

PREPARATION

Obtain a wide selection of records or tapes. Include the widest possible range of tastes — old, recent, classical and popular music. Record short extracts from each, leaving a short gap between each recording. Compile a list of questions concerning each recording. Make the questions as varied as possible. Include the name of the piece, the singer, who wrote the lyrics and other information which can be found on the record sleeve.

ACTION

Seat the group so that everyone can hear clearly. Play the first recording and then ask the questions concerning it. Have the players write down the answers. Before continuing with the next recording, players can call out their answers. Alternatively, go through the complete quiz, then return to the beginning of the tape and replay each piece before people call out the answers they have written down. When answers are given, ensure that ample time is allowed to discuss each piece of music and for players to express their opinions.

COMMENT

Recording a musical quiz is very time-consuming. However, it provides an excellent quiz, giving plenty of opportunity for group discussion and interaction. Once recorded, it can be used many times with different groups.

SUBJECT AND ASSOCIATION

MATERIALS

None.

PREPARATION

None.

ACTION

Ask two players to leave the group and go into an adjoining room. While out of the room they think of a subject and something associated with it. Examples:

King Arthur	The Round Table
Kojak	Lollipops
Alice	A looking glass
The Owl and the Pussycat	A pea-green boat

Having thought of a subject and its association, the players decide which of them is to represent the subject and which the association. The two players then return to the group. They are asked questions to enable the group to discover what they represent. The questions should be phrased in a manner which allows the answers to be 'Yes' or 'No'. One partner may not answer questions concerning the subject or association the other person represents. Allow an allotted time or limit the number of questions so that couples have the opportunity of beating the group. When the subject and association have been guessed, ask another couple to leave the room. This continues until all the players have had an opportunity to be subject and association.

VARIATION

Play as a team game, giving members from opposing teams turns at thinking up the subject and association.

COMMENT

If some players find it difficult to think up their own subject and association, write out a selection of these which the couples can then draw from a bag.

BASEBALL QUIZ

MATERIALS

Chalk or newspaper and a quiz book.

PREPARATION

Compile a list of general knowledge questions or obtain a quiz book. Mark out a baseball diamond with chalk, as shown in *Figure 8.1*, or place sheets of newspaper to represent the bases. Chairs can also be used, if required, for the less able.

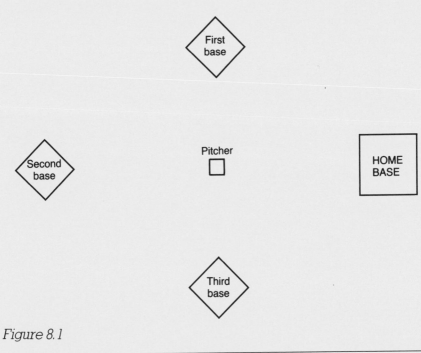

Figure 8.1

ACTION

Divide the group into two teams. Act as umpire and pitcher or delegate this responsibility to a player. The pitcher or questioner stands in the centre and pitches a question to the first player of the team which is batting. If he answers wrongly, he is out and the next player in that team takes a turn at batting. If he answers correctly, he proceeds to first base. When there is someone already at first base that person proceeds to second base. Each player's object is to return to home base. Any participant batting who answers wrongly is out and any person at that time on first, second or third base remains where he is. The game continues in this manner until three players are out. The other team then takes a turn at batting. Every time a player reaches home base a point is scored for his team.

COMMENT

Using basic baseball rules for the basis of a quiz provides novelty and also introduces some physical movement during the activity. It is also a useful format to employ out of doors on a nice day.

EXERCISE YOUR WORD POWER

A selection of stimulating word-games

BEGINNINGS AND ENDINGS

MATERIALS

Pencils and paper.

PREPARATION

None.

ACTION

Give each player a pencil and paper. Instruct them to write the letters of the alphabet down the left hand side of the paper, omitting the more difficult letters like Q, X, Y and Z. Explain that each person must think of words which begin and end with each letter. Here are a few examples:

A— AGORAPHOBIA	D— DEMOLISHED
B— BATHTUB	E— EARTHQUAKE
C— CONCENTRIC	F— FIREPROOF

The object is to think of the longest words. Allow ten to fifteen minutes and then ask the players to call out the words. A point can be scored for each letter in the words. The player with the most points wins.

VARIATIONS

1 Instruct each person to write down as many words as they can think of beginning and ending with a given letter. The person with the most words at the end of a pre-set time wins.

2 Players write down any words that begin and end with the same letter, but for each word the letter may be different. The person with the longest list wins.

COMMENT

Take the opportunity to discuss the meaning of any unusual words which are used. A dictionary will also be handy to check any words which are doubtful.

HALF-AND-HALF

MATERIALS

Blackboard and chalk.

PREPARATION

None.

ACTION

Seat the players in front of a blackboard. Have a participant write the first syllable of a two-syllable word of his choice on the blackboard without stating the word. This could be 'son'. The next player thinks of an ending for the word and writes it on the board. In this case he may think of 'net', making the word 'sonnet'. Here are examples of some more words which can be used:

red-uce	rub-ber	fore-arm
sen-ate	mal-let	tal-ent
de-pot	woe-ful	cra-dle
tre-mor	fri-gate	but-tress

There are thousands more. The game continues in this fashion.

Make sure that there are an odd number of people in the game to ensure that the same players do not start the word each time around.

If a player cannot complete a word then a point can be awarded to the person who started it. If he does complete it, he gains a point. Players may challenge each other if they think someone has not a proper word in mind when the first part is written up. If the challenge is successful, the challenger gains two points. If not, the other player gains two points. Alternatively, disqualify players who write nonsensical beginnings.

VARIATION

Play as a team game with team members conferring and challenging the opposing team.

COMMENT

A stimulating game which motivates quick thinking, promotes interaction and can help break down social isolation.

196

STAIRWAY OF WORDS

MATERIALS

Pencils, paper, scissors and a small bag.

PREPARATION

Using small squares of paper, equal to the number of participants, write on each a letter of the alphabet and place them in a bag. Avoid the more difficult letters like Q, X, Y and Z. Instead, pick letters which can easily be made into a two-letter word by the addition of another letter.

ACTION

Give out pencils and paper. Ask one player to pick a letter out of the bag. (Alternatively, have a player call out a letter of the alphabet.) Instruct participants to form a stairway of different words beginning with the chosen letter, and adding an extra letter each time to form steps. Here is an example:

A
AN
ATE
ABLE
ACTOR
ABATED
ABANDON
ABDUCTED
ACCESSORY
ADJUDICATE
AGGRAVATING
ALLITERATION

The person who forms the longest stairway wins. Then ask someone else to choose another letter from the bag and proceed as before.

VARIATIONS

Instead of using pencils and paper, write the first letter on the blackboard, then ask a player to write up the first step of the stairway. The person next to him writes up the second step and so on until no more steps can be added. Players who become stuck can have help from other players who may give clues to the words. If no more steps can be added, the next player starts a new stairway off by putting another first letter on the blackboard.

COMMENT

Take opportunities to discuss the meanings of unusual words which are used. A dictionary will be handy for this purpose and for establishing correct spellings.

SPELLMASTER

MATERIALS

Card and a magic marker.

PREPARATION

Cut out forty-six cards measuring about six inches square. Using a magic marker make two sets of alphabet cards, one letter per card, leaving out the letters Q, X and Z. Also prepare a list of words which do not contain double or repeated letters. Ensure that the first few words are fairly easy. Here are a few examples:

imply	vertigo	tangible
space	improve	chair
stake	overhang	table

ACTION

Divide the players into two groups. Give out a set of alphabet cards to each team. Depending on the number of players, some people may have more than one card. Form the teams into two lines facing each other but keeping them some distance apart. Call out the first word on your list. The players holding the appropriate letters stand one pace forward and arrange themselves to show the letters of the word in the correct order. Any player with more than one letter of the word passes them along the line so they can be held up in their proper positions. The first team to do so wins a point. The game continues in this manner.

COMMENT

An amusing game which provides light movement.

FIND THE WORD

MATERIALS

None.

PREPARATION

None.

ACTION

Seat the players in a circle. Ask for a volunteer to leave the room. While he is out, the remaining players think of a word which contains five or more letters. The exiled person is called back into the room and puts questions to players, one question to a participant. The answer must include the word decided upon. Here is an example, using the word 'changed':

Question   "Have you always lived in this country?"

Answer   "Yes, but we have changed addresses many times."

Question   "What did you have for dinner last night?"

Answer   "We've changed our eating habits and no longer eat at night."

Question   "Where did you go for your last holiday?"

Answer   "We flew out to Austria and then changed to a coach to go on to Germany."

The object of the game is for the questioner to guess the word the players decided to use. When he has discovered it another player is asked to leave the room and the game continues in the same manner.

VARIATIONS

Have the players think of a proverb, saying or a quotation. Each person is then allotted a word from the proverb and must include this in his answer when questioned. This can be quite difficult for individual questioners to guess. Try having two or three people leave the room together. When they return they can act as a team.

COMMENT

If some players find the questioning and answering a little difficult, omit this part of the procedure and have the players in the circle, when named, simply state a sentence which includes the chosen word.

COMBINATIONS

MATERIALS

Pencils and paper.

PREPARATION

Make up fifteen combinations of letters: five of two letters, five of three letters and five of four letters. Here is an example:

AN	ACH	PATH
CH	STA	DURA
BR	BRA	BREA
OU	TRI	PART
ME	AND	ANGE

ACTION

Give players pencils and paper and ask them to write down the longest words they can think of which contain the combinations — one per word. Examples:

AN   — AB*AN*DON

ACH   — S*ACH*ET

PATH   — SYM*PATH*IZE

The combinations must not be placed at the beginning or at the end of any words. Players score a point for each letter in the words. After a given time stop players writing and, taking the combinations one at a time, have them call out their words.

VARIATION

Divide the group into teams of three or four players and have each team compete in turn.

COMMENT

You can, of course, use more than fifteen combinations to make the game last longer. Have a dictionary at hand for reference and take opportunities to discuss the meaning of words which are not familiar to everyone in the group.

TABOO

MATERIALS

None.

PREPARATION

None.

ACTION

Seat the players in a circle and decide on a word or words which will be taboo. A short, simple word such as 'yes', 'no', 'you', 'I', 'the', 'is', 'an', 'at', 'of', 'to', 'he' or 'she', is ideal. Ask for a volunteer to go into the centre of the circle. This person approaches players in turn and asks them questions. His object is to try to make the person being questioned say the taboo word. He may not question any player for longer than a pre-set time — say, one or two minutes — at any one attempt. Players must answer the questions with a proper sentence as quickly as possible. If the forbidden word is said then that person becomes the questioner. The taboo word can also be changed when a new questioner takes over.

COMMENT

A simple, amusing game, but one in which concentration and quick thinking is needed.

KEY WORD

MATERIALS

Pencils and paper.

PREPARATION

Think up a selection of key words which can be built into longer words. Examples:

weak	love	as	own
head	one	it	act
self	do	us	out

ACTION

Hand out pencils and paper. Write a key word on the blackboard or call one out for players to note. Instruct them to write down as many words as they can think of which contain that word. Here are some examples using the word 'love':

beloved	foxglove	pullover
lover	slovenly	lovelorn
lovely	lovelier	loveless
lovebird	loveliest	loveliness

After a set time, have the players shout out the words and allow points for original words which no one else has thought of. Choose another key word and continue as before.

VARIATION

Rather than have each player write down the words, work round the group, each player writing an additional word on the blackboard. Allow players to assist those who become stuck by giving clues to or miming the meaning of another word.

COMMENT

This is another game which is very easy to play and can be used to encourage participation, improve concentration and help build confidence.

LONG WORDS

MATERIALS

Pencils and paper.

PREPARATION

Think of a long word, such as 'administrative', 'differential', 'circum-navigate' or 'comprehensible'.

ACTION

Give the players pencils and paper. Write one of the above words, or one of your own, on a blackboard. Instruct each person to write down as many words as possible, of four letters or more, using the letters from the word written on the blackboard. If 'administrative' was used a player might write:

native	drive	nest
stride	vest	date
raid	strait	strata
mist	data	dent
trite	admire	strive
read	risen	dire
start	irate	rave

There are many more words. Allow about ten minutes, then have the players call out the words listed. The winner is either the person with the most words or the player who has constructed the most words not used by others.

VARIATION

Write the long word on the blackboard and, as players think of words, instruct them to write the words on the blackboard themselves.

COMMENT

A word game in which it is easy to participate and which is also a good ice-breaker.

ADJECTIVES

MATERIALS

Pencils and paper.

PREPARATION

Copy-type a passage from a book, magazine or newspaper, but leave blank spaces in place of all the adjectives. Have the typed sheet photocopied.

ACTION

Give each player a copy of the passage. Explain that an adjective is a 'describing' word, added to a noun or pronoun to describe it more fully. An example is: A <u>full</u> moon shone onto the <u>wide</u>, <u>silent</u> lake. The words underlined are adjectives. Once everyone knows what an adjective is, request that they fill in the blank spaces with adjectives of their own. When completed, have each player read out their version. End by reading out the original. Encourage the creation of fun and have a vote for the most colourful or absurd passage.

VARIATIONS

1   Add a jumbled list of the original adjectives used in the passage to the sheet given to the players. They must place them in the correct blanks.
2   Provide your own list of colourful adjectives, or write a list at random on the blackboard, from which the players must fill in the blank spaces.

COMMENT

Romantic novels or stories provide a rich source of material for this game.

CATEGORY CHALLENGE

MATERIALS

None.

PREPARATION

Make a long list of categories. Here are some:

birds	cities	cathedrals
fish	trees	books
vegetables	oceans	explorers
counties	rivers	famous sailors
foods	countries	politicians
animals	lakes	presidents
TV programmes	types of car	authors
painters	footballers	flowers

ACTION

Divide the group into two teams, and toss a coin to see which side goes first. Decide on an initial category and announce it. The first team shouts out the name of something belonging to the decided category, then the opposing players do likewise. This continues, alternating between teams, until there is a pause of longer than fifteen seconds. The other players are then awarded a point and the game is continued, using a new category. The team with the most points at the end wins.

VARIATION

Form the players into a circle and call out a category. Players take it in turns to shout the name of something in the category. When a player fails he can be knocked out of the game. The person who remains 'in' the longest wins.

COMMENT

So that the game does not last too long, a few difficult categories can be included in your list.

FIVE-WORD CHALLENGE

MATERIALS

None.

PREPARATION

None.

ACTION

Seat the players in a circle. One person (A) calls out someone else's name and says a five-letter word like 'dress'. The player named (B) then states five other words beginning with the individual letters of the word called out by A. In the case of the example 'dress' the named player might say:

(D)   drunk

(R)   ripe

(E)   express

(S)   sausage

(S)   saw

If player B fails to do this within a given time-limit — say, thirty seconds — he must call out another person's name and another five-letter word. If B succeeds in getting the five words, player A begins again, calling out another name and a five-letter word. The game continues in this fashion. Encourage players to call out the names of people who have not had a turn.

VARIATIONS

Make the game easier or more difficult by decreasing or increasing the number of letters in the word called out.

COMMENT

A game which is fun and stimulates quick thinking. It also enables players to learn each other's names. If they do not know the names, have them enquire of each other.

VOCABULARY

MATERIALS

Pencils, paper, card and scissors.

PREPARATION

Cut out two-inch squares of card equal to the number of players. Write a different letter of the alphabet on each card. Do not use Q, X, Y or Z.

ACTION

Seat the players in a circle. Give each person a pencil, some paper and one of the alphabet cards. The cards can be handed out at random or players allowed to pick one each. Tell people that they have one or two minutes to write down as many words as they can think of beginning with their letter. When the two minutes are up, the letter cards are passed on to the person on the left and another period given to write as many words as possible. The procedure continues in this fashion until every player has had all the letters. Taking a letter at a time, players now call out the words written down. Whoever has the most words for a given letter wins that round and whoever has the most words overall is vocabulary champion.

VARIATIONS

1 To shorten the length of time needed for the game, pick out only a few letters from the alphabet cards, call out each one separately and have all players write the words at the same time. Alternatively participants can shout out the letters at random.
2 Use only one letter of the alphabet but allow five or ten minutes for the word list to be compiled.

COMMENT

In this game, good opportunities to discuss the meaning and use of words present themselves. To make the game more difficult, stipulate that words of more than four, five or six letters must be used. Also, exclude the use of proper names or nouns and plurals.

PASS THE RHYME

MATERIALS

None.

PREPARATION

None.

ACTION

Seat the players in a circle. The procedure is begun by someone asking a question like: "Have you seen my hat?". The next person must begin a statement with a word that rhymes with the last word of the question. This may be: "Pat the dog this way!" Another player proceeds: "Hay is made at this time of year." And yet another participant: "Clear is the sky above." The game continues in this fashion round the circle. Each individual statement must make sense. Encourage players to respond reasonably quickly. When a player cannot think of another statement beginning with a word which rhymes with the last word of the previous sentence, he begins the cycle again by asking another question.

VARIATION

A player starts the game by saying a word. The person next to him continues with another word which rhymes with it: 'Hat, fat, that, mat', and so on. When a player cannot think of another word which rhymes he starts the procedure again with a new word.

COMMENT

The rhyming statements are quite difficult. If the group is new and not very confident, practise by using the variation before attempting the statements.

MATERIALS

Pencils and paper. A blackboard or a large sheet of paper.

PREPARATION

Using any letters of the alphabet, make up a jumbled word square, as shown in *Figure 9.1*. Make sure that one or two words are fairly obvious and that a large number of words can be formed from the letters, as instructed below. Letters can be repeated.

C	A	N	D
O	L	O	O
D	E	A	N
L	O	D	E

Figure 9.1

ACTION

Give the players pencils and paper. Instruct them to form as many words of four letters or more as they can from the letters in the squares. The letters in each word must always be adjacent across, down, up or diagonal to the previous letter. Here are some examples from *Figure 9.1* above:

DONE	LONDON	CANON	LOAD	CLAD
LODE	LEAN	CLONE	DALE	NONE
LADEN	DEAL	COLD	LEAD	ALONE
COAL	NOON	LAND	DOLE	COLON

Many more words can be formed. At the end of a given time have players call out their words. Have a points system, perhaps one point for each word and an extra point for an original word that no one else has. The player with the most points wins.

COMMENT

To make the game easier, include three-letter words. A number of these games can be made up and photocopied so that sheets can be handed out when required. Once copied, a supply can be kept for constant use.

CHANGE THE WORD

MATERIALS

Pencils and paper.

PREPARATION

None.

ACTION

Give players pencils and paper, then ask them to call out a word. Everyone writes down the same word at the top of their paper. In the example given this word is ACE. Request another word with the same number of letters — BOW in the example. This is written lower down, leaving a gap on the paper. Now instruct each person to change the top word (ACE) into the bottom word (BOW) in as few steps as possible. Only one letter can be changed at a time, but the order of the letters can be varied. Each step must form a complete word. Here is an example:

Beginning word	ACE
Step 1	CAW
Step 2	COW
Final word	BOW

The player who uses the fewest number of steps to make the change wins that particular round. Continue the game with two new words.

VARIATION

Divide the group into small teams and have the teams compete.

COMMENT

This is not as easy as it appears. Start by using three-letter words. After some practice, advance to four-, five- or six-letter words.

WORD BUILDING

MATERIALS

Blackboard and chalk.

PREPARATION

None.

ACTION

Seat the players in a circle. Ask one player to think of a word which contains two or more letters. Without saying what the word is, the person writes the first letter of his word on the blackboard. The player next to him now thinks of a word with three or more letters in it which contains the letter already written on the board. He adds a letter from his word, putting it either before or after the letter already on the blackboard, ensuring that it does not form a complete word. Players, in turn, add an additional letter, each time thinking of a new word, but avoiding completing the word on the blackboard. A game might go like this:

	Word in mind	Letter added
First player	magic	M
Second player	married	MA
Third player	imagine	IMA
Fourth player	climate	LIMA
Fifth player	sublimate	BLIMA

And so the game continues. Each player must have a word in mind and can be challenged by any other player if this is in doubt. Should the challenger be wrong he has a point scored against him. If he was correct in his assumption, the player who was bluffing loses a point. As the object is to avoid completing a word, any player who does so also has a point scored against him. The person who has the least penalty points at the end of the game is the winner.

COMMENT

A game to motivate quick thinking, help to break down social isolation and increase word power.

LONG SENTENCES

MATERIALS

Pencils and paper.

PREPARATION

None.

ACTION

Issue players with pencils and paper. Instruct them to write as long a sentence as possible on any subject, but no word should contain more than five letters. The sentence can be comic but must follow some sort of logic or sense. Here is an example:

'Who was the girl with the long hair, blue eyes, big feet and nails like claws, who you were seen with down by the lake last night when it was dark and eerie, and the man went to find you, but you ran away?'

Allow five or ten minutes and then ask each player to read out his sentence. Whoever produces the longest sentence can be the winner. Alternatively, vote for the best sentence or the most comic effect.

VARIATIONS

1 Players write the longest sentence they can compile, using words with no more than four letters.
2 This time, players use no more than three letters in a word.

COMMENT

A game to stimulate imaginative thinking. Combine the variations and have rounds using up to five letters in a word, then four letters and finish with three-letter word sentences.

CONCEALED WORDS

MATERIALS

A book, pencils and paper.

PREPARATION

Type out a fairly long extract from a well-known book or poem and have it photocopied.

ACTION

Give each player a copy of the extract and a pencil. Instruct them to find as many concealed words, formed within words or combining parts of two or more adjoining words, as possible. Here is an example taken at random from *The Woman in White* by Wilkie Collins. Some of the concealed words are underlined.

'What could I do? Here was a stranger utterly and helplessly at my mercy — and that stranger a forlorn woman. No house was near; no one was passing whom I could consult; and no earthly right existed on my part to give me power of control over her, even if I had known how to exercise it. I trace these lines, self-distrustfully, with the shadows of after-events darkening the very paper I write on; and still I say, what could I do?'

The person with the longest list of words wins.

VARIATIONS

To make the game easier, use a poem. Number each line and ask players to find a particular word in each line to which a clue is given. As an example, here are the first two lines of Rupert Brooke's poem, *The Soldier.*

1 If I should die, think only this of me:
2 That there's some corner of a foreign field
   Clues: 1 Lives in water.
          2 Period of royal rule.

COMMENT

As well as being good fun this game can be an excellent way to introduce discussion about particular books or poems.

WHAT DOES IT MEAN?

MATERIALS

A dictionary.

PREPARATION

Compile a list of words, some fairly easy and others more difficult, and their meanings. Examples:

ABYSS — a bottomless chasm, a deep gorge; an immeasurable depth.

EPIGRAM — a short poem with a witty, pointed ending; a saying.

DROWSY — sleepy, dozy, sluggish.

INCIPIENT — beginning; at the first stage.

LIMBO — a condition of neglect; prison, confinement.

ACTION

Divide the group into two or more teams. The teams, in turn, are given a word from the previously prepared list. If a team answers with the correct meaning, a point is scored. If they fail to come up with the meaning, the word may be offered to the other team(s) for a bonus point. The team which scores the most points wins.

VARIATIONS

1   Give several meanings for each word listed; the teams, or individuals, must decide which meaning is correct. For example:

RATIFY — excuse, please, confirm, originate. (Answer: confirm.)

COY — shy, brash, embarrassed, backward. (Answer: shy.)

SUBVERT — overturn, disgrace, stifle, speak out. (Answer: overturn.)

2   Using a dictionary of English or contemporary slang, compile a list of slang, with meanings, then proceed as above. Examples:

FULL OF BEANS — enthusiastic, excited, cheerful.

JUMP THE GUN — act prematurely.

HANG LOOSE — relax, take things as they come.

COMMENT

An excellent game for increasing word power, discussing the use and learning the meaning of words which occur frequently. We usually guess at their meanings without bothering to look them up. The lists can be compiled to suit the word range of any group.

OUT AND ABOUT

Outdoor activities

MAT-TOSSING RACE

MATERIALS

A tennis racket, a beer- or rubber mat for each team and two ropes.

PREPARATION

Mark out a course with the two ropes across it some twenty to thirty feet apart as shown in *Figure 10.1*. The ropes can be attached to trees, posts or players can hold them. If the participants are agile then keep the ropes slightly below shoulder height, otherwise they are best at shoulder height or slightly higher.

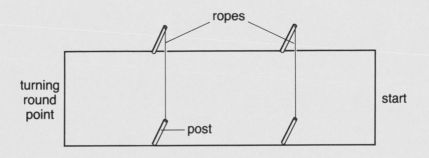

Figure 10.1

ACTION

Divide the group into two or more teams. The first player in each team is given a tennis racket and a beer-mat. Players hold the rackets out and place a mat on it. On the word 'go' they proceed to the first rope, toss the mat over the top of it and catch it again on the other side. Players must keep trying until they succeed in catching the mat on the tennis racket before going on to the next rope. When the far end of the course is reached, the players turn around and follow the same procedure on the way back. On returning to the starting-point, the second player in each team takes the tennis racket and beer-mat and attempts the course. The first team finished wins.

VARIATIONS

1 To make the game more difficult for players who are agile, replace the tennis racket with a table tennis bat and/or the beer-mat with a ball.

2 Slow the game down by having members complete the course one by one. Give points for making it back to the start without dropping the mat, for the fastest time, and penalty points each time the mat is dropped. The player with the most points after the course has been attempted two or three times is the winner.

3 For novelty, on Shrove Tuesday, replace the tennis racket with a light frying-pan and the mat with a pancake.

COMMENT

This is a hilarious activity which provides much laughter and breaks down barriers.

PLATE-SKIMMING OLYMPICS

MATERIALS

A supply of paper plates and a tape measure.

PREPARATION

None.

ACTION

Mark a toe line. Give the first player three paper plates which he throws or skims through the air, one at a time, as far as possible. The distance of the best throw is measured. The place where the plate actually ends up is the distance measured and not where it first lands and bounces. The next player then throws three plates and so on. Make the competition the best of three rounds.

COMMENT

A simple but entertaining activity in which everyone can take part.

REVERSE RELAY RACE

MATERIALS

None.

PREPARATION

Mark out a starting-line and another point some twenty to thirty yards away.

ACTION

Divide the group into two teams. Team members then split into pairs. The first couple in each team line up on the starting-line, partners facing in opposite directions and linking arms. On the word 'go' the players begin walking — one facing forward and the other walking backwards — to the point about thirty yards away. The couples then turn around and, reversing roles, return to the start. The second couple in each team then link arms and begin walking. The first team to complete the course wins.

VARIATION

Use this game as a short activity for fun by forming the group into couples and see who are the first two back to the starting-point.

COMMENT

Walking is recommended, but if the players are young and agile they can speed up the action by running.

ONE-MINUTE WALK

MATERIALS

A watch to judge the time.

PREPARATION

None.

ACTION

Stand all the players in a straight line facing the same way. Mark a finishing point some fifty to a hundred yards away. Tell everyone that they are to begin walking on the word 'go' and walk to the finishing line in one minute. Once the contest is started, players must keep walking forward until the minute is up. If they reach the finish before the time is up they cannot stop but must keep going. Neither can they turn round. No one is allowed to remain still until the time is up. When it is, the person nearest the finishing line is declared the winner.

COMMENT

A gentle game in which all ages can compete on equal terms. Let players have two or three attempts, but change the length of time to be taken and/or the distance to be covered.

RINGS ON A STICK

MATERIALS

Ten rings made from rubber, cane or rope and two sticks or pieces of thick cane.

PREPARATION

None.

ACTION

Divide the group into two teams and lay five rings in a row for each team. Give a player from each team a stick or cane and instruct them to pick the rings up using only the stick. The rings must be picked up one at a time until all five are on the stick. The player who accomplishes the task in the quickest time wins a point for his team. Another person from each team then attempts the task. The team which accumulates the most points can be declared the winner.

COMMENT

An activity which is fun, but not as easy as it appears. The first ring is easy to lift but the remainder are more difficult.

MATERIALS

Ten empty washing-up liquid bottles, some sand or earth and two balls — tennis balls will do — and a table.

PREPARATION

Part-fill the washing-up liquid bottles with sand — about a quarter-full should suffice — and seal them.

ACTION

Set the bottles up as for tenpin bowls, as shown in *Figure 10.2*. Place a table or bench on its side several feet behind the pins so that when the balls are thrown it will act as a barrier to stop them. Mark a bowling line about twelve to fourteen feet in front of the pins. Give the first player two balls and see if he can bowl all the pins down. Two balls bowled is a frame.

If all the pins are knocked down with the first ball bowled, it is called a strike. A strike scores ten points plus the score from the same player's next frame, added on as extra points. If ten pins are knocked over by two balls thrown it is called a spare. A spare scores ten points plus the score from the first ball thrown during the same player's next frame. A game usually comprises ten frames.

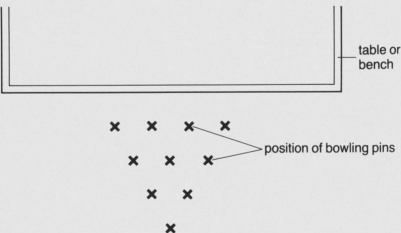

table or bench

position of bowling pins

Figure 10.2

It will be necessary to have players take turns at setting up the pins and throwing the balls back to the bowling line. Scores can be recorded on a blackboard, or players given paper and pencils to keep a record of their own score.

VARIATIONS

1 *Sudden Death* This is an elimination game of bowls. The pins are set up for the first player. One or more balls can be used for a frame. When the first person bowls, any pins which have been knocked down stay down. If any remain standing, the next player must try to knock one or more pins down, but if he misses he is eliminated from the game and another player tries. When all the pins have been knocked down they are set up again. The game continues in this fashion until only one player is left and he is declared the winner.

2 *Novelty Bowls* The rules are the same as for ordinary bowls or *Sudden Death* but each time a player bowls he must do so in a different manner. Examples:
   1 Using his left hand.
   2 With one eye closed.
   3 Standing with his back to the pins.
   4 Standing on one leg.
   5 Standing sideways.

COMMENT

Bowls are always popular and provide light exercise, opportunity for interaction and satisfying relaxation. Once the basic equipment is made up for the game it can be kept and used again and again. The game can also be played indoors in a large room. However, be careful of any windows in the line of fire, should anyone bowl extra hard!

THREE-LEGGED RACE

MATERIALS

Lengths of material to tie players' legs together.

PREPARATION

None.

ACTION

Mark out a starting-point and a finishing line about fifty feet away. Form the group into two teams. Players choose a partner from their own teams and one person's right leg is tied to his partner's left leg with a length of material. Teams are lined up at the starting-point. On the word 'go' the first couple from each team head for the finishing line. When they have reached it the second couple in their team can begin the course. The first team finished is the winner.

COMMENT

It helps to give a demonstration and have a short practice for everyone before beginning the race. Also emphasise that it is easier if taken at a steady pace and not rushed.

SILLY WALKS COMPETITION

MATERIALS

None.

PREPARATION

None.

ACTION

Mark out two lines about fifteen feet apart. Stand the players behind one of the lines. Ask participants, one at a time, to walk from one line to the other; each person must walk in an individual manner. Players may walk:

backwards	forwards
with hands in the air	on tip-toe
sideways	hopping on one leg
using a hop, skip and jump	using long strides
hopping on two legs	two steps forward, one back

End by having a vote to select the silliest walk.

VARIATION

Split the players into teams of two or three people. Each team is given a few minutes to invent a silly walk. They take turns to demonstrate by crossing between the lines, people in the team performing the walk action together.

COMMENT

A game to encourage invention and which provides no end of fun.

MATERIALS

Some small cardboard boxes, barrel biscuit tins, jam jars, golf clubs and golf balls.

PREPARATION

Lay out a ten- or twelve-hole miniature golf course using all or any of the containers mentioned above. Number and place them on their sides with one end open.

ACTION

Give the first player a golf club and ball and see how many strokes are needed to place the ball in the first hole. Player number two then tries. And so the game continues until all the players have had a go. Attention is then centred on hole number two. Players keep count of strokes taken at each hole or have a scorer recording them on a score sheet. The person with the least number of strokes overall is the winner.

VARIATIONS

1   Place obstacles between the teeing-off spot and the holes. Use bricks, sacking or anything else to hand which will obstruct the path of the ball.

2   Split the players into small groups of three or four people. The first group play for hole number one. This time each person only has one go at placing the ball in the hole. If no one succeeds, everyone makes another attempt and so on. The object for each player is to be the first to get the ball into the hole. When this has been achieved they move on to hole number two and another group try for hole number one. The person in each group who wins the most holes is champion. Have a final game in which all the winners from the first round challenge each other to see who is supreme champion.

COMMENT

This activity provides light exercise, entertainment and is a relaxing way to spend time on a pleasant day.

BALL-THROWING CONTEST

MATERIALS

A tennis ball.

PREPARATION

None.

ACTION

The group is formed into two teams who stand in line about ten feet apart with opposing players facing each other. A tennis ball is given to one team leader at the end of his line. He throws the ball to the opposing player opposite him who must catch it one-handed and throw it back. By this time the person who initially threw the ball will have vacated his place in line and gone to the other end. His place will have been taken by player number two in his line who catches the ball and throws it again to the second player in the opposing team. And so the game continues. Anyone who drops the ball loses a point for his team. Have a time-limit for play. The team which loses the least points wins.

COMMENT

Should players have difficulty catching the tennis ball one-handed, use a larger soft ball and allow the players to catch it with both hands. As an added novelty use a hard-boiled egg instead of a ball.

BALLOON BALL

MATERIALS

Some balloons or a large sponge ball.

PREPARATION

Mark out the boundaries of a pitch. Ideally, it should be forty feet long by twenty feet wide. The goals should be eight to ten feet wide. However, a smaller pitch would be suitable.

ACTION

Two teams are selected. Teams need have no specific number of players, but five to ten is desirable. Before play begins, emphasise the following rules:

1   The balloon may only be hit by the flat of the hand.
2   There will be no pushing, shoving, kicking or rough play.
3   The balloon cannot be held in the hands. It can only be bounced or patted.
4   To score, the balloon must pass through the goal below waist level.
5   If the balloon goes over the side lines it is thrown into play by a member of the opposing team.

Decide which direction each team is to play, then start the game in the centre by tapping the balloon into the air. When a goal is scored, the goalkeeper pats the balloon into play. After five to ten minutes have a short break and change the direction of play. The team scoring the most goals wins.

COMMENT

It is a good idea not to have everyone in the group playing at the same time. Keep two or three people in reserve for each team. If anyone tires or becomes winded players can then be substituted. To slow the pace of the game, include a ruling that players must walk. This can be quite an energetic game and is best played in some shade or on a dullish day for those who are not too fit.

NEWSPAPER CHASE

MATERIALS

A rolled-up newspaper.

PREPARATION

None.

ACTION

Have the players stand in a circle with a two- to three-foot space between them and their hands behind their backs. One player walks around the circle on the outside carrying a rolled-up newspaper. He suddenly places the newspaper in the hands of someone he chooses in the circle. He then runs all the way round the circle pursued by the person now in possession of the newspaper. He tries to get back to the vacated place in the circle before that person can catch him up and touch him with the newspaper. If he fails, he takes back the newspaper, remains outside the circle and tries again. If he suc-ceeds, the person who chased him walks around the circle with the newspaper and places it in someone else's hands. The game continues in this manner.

COMMENT

A game which provides good physical exercise. If necessary, slow the game down by ruling that players must walk around the circle at all times and not run.

DRAGGING THE BALL

MATERIALS

A long rope (skipping ropes are excellent) and a large rubber ball for each team.

PREPARATION

None.

ACTION

Mark a starting line and place a chair or some object about thirty feet away. Form the group into two or more teams and line them up at the starting-point. Give the first player in each team a ball and rope. On a given word the players, holding both ends of the rope, use it to drag the ball the length of the course and back again. When they return to the starting-point the next player in the team takes over. The game continues in this manner until each player has taken part. The first team finished is declared the winner.

COMMENT

This is really good fun and is a game which can be paced to suit most people. The more uneven the lawn chosen to play on the better.

CLOCK CROQUET

MATERIALS

Twelve wooden pegs, a croquet or hockey ball, a wooden mallet and a heavy hammer.

PREPARATION

Hammer the pegs into the ground in a circle which has a circumference of about twenty to thirty feet. The pegs should be equal distances apart so that they resemble the hour figures of a clock, as shown in *Figure 10.3*. Mark a spot inside the circle which is at least four feet from the circumference but not in the centre.

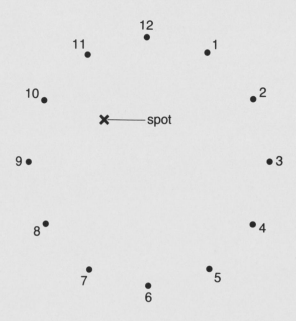

Figure 10.3

ACTION

The first player places the ball on the spot and using the mallet strikes the ball — croquet style — aiming to hit peg number one. The number of strikes required to achieve this is recorded. Another player then takes over and tries to hit peg number one with the ball. When everyone has had a turn, attention is given to peg number two, and so on, around the clock. The player with the lowest number of strikes overall is the winner.

VARIATION

Instead of wooden pegs, use metal or wire loops. Players must then pass the ball through the loops.

COMMENT

This activity provides gentle exercise, relaxation, opportunity for interaction and is very enjoyable on a nice day.

CHARLIE CHAPLIN RELAY

MATERIALS

Some balloons or balls, books and walking-sticks or canes, equal to the number of teams.

PREPARATION

None.

ACTION

Mark out a starting-point and a course about twenty-five feet long. Divide the group into teams and line them up at the starting-point. Give the first person in each team a ball, a book and a cane. Instruct them to place the ball between their knees, balance the book on their heads and grasp the cane in one hand. The players walk the course, keeping the ball between their knees, the book on their heads and twirling the cane, Charlie Chaplin style. If an object is dropped it must be picked up and replaced before the player continues. Once he has made it back to the starting-point the next player in line has a turn. The first team to complete the course wins.

COMMENT

Make sure that there is plenty of space between teams so that players are not struck by twirling canes when in pursuit of dropped objects. The game can also be played indoors in a large room with a high ceiling. If balancing the book on their heads is too difficult omit this or, alternatively, omit the balloon-between-knees part.

HAND TENNIS

MATERIALS

A large sponge ball, a softball or a tennis ball and a net or rope.

PREPARATION

Stretch the net between trees or posts and mark out boundaries as for tennis.

ACTION

Teams may comprise any number of players but six to eight is ideal. The object is for each team to bat the ball over the net, keeping it within the agreed boundaries or court by using only the palms of their hands. Ensure that the following rules are understood:

1   The ball is in play as long as it bounces. If it rolls, goes out of court, into or under the net, it is 'dead' and must be served again for play to continue.

2   The ball is served from the back of the playing area. Each player in the team must take a turn at serving.

3   The ball can go from player to player in the same team before being returned over the net to the opposing team.

Scoring can be (a) as in tennis; (b) by deciding a number of points to be scored before the game begins. A longer game is achieved by only allowing points to be scored by whichever team is serving when the ball is in play. When the rules are understood, toss a coin to decide which team serves first.

COMMENT

Make the contest the best of three games, alternating the direction of play for each game. If there are lots of players form several teams and have an elimination tournament. Playing time can be shortened by reducing the score needed to win each game.

GARDEN BOWLS

MATERIALS

A golf ball and tennis balls equal to the number of players.

PREPARATION

None.

ACTION

A player bowls the golf ball from a drawn line. This ball is called a 'jack'. Each player now bowls a tennis ball in turn, trying to place it as close as possible to the jack. The person who comes closest wins a point. The jack is bowled once more and the same procedure gone through again. The first player to reach a previously agreed number of points — this can be ten, fifteen or twenty — wins. Scores can be kept by individuals or recorded on a sheet of paper or blackboard.

VARIATION

If there are a lot of players split them into groups of four or five people. The winners from each group can have a final game to decide who is champion.

COMMENT

A delightful game which provides light exercise, entertainment, relaxation and opportunity for interaction.

BUCKET BRIGADE

MATERIALS

Two buckets of water, two plastic or paper cups, a jar or bottle with a narrow neck which will hold at least a quart of water and two small tables. Also some towels may come in handy!

PREPARATION

None.

ACTION

The group is divided into two teams and formed into two lines, players standing one behind the other. Place a bucket of water at the front of each team and the quart bottle or jar on a small table behind the last player. Give the first player in each team a plastic cup. On the word 'go' these players fill their cups with water and pass them back along the line until they reach the last players. The end players pour what water is left in the cups into quart bottles, run to the front with the empty cups, refill them again from the buckets and pass them backwards. The first team to fill their quart bottle with water is declared the winner.

COMMENT

A super game for a warm summer day.

STEPPING OUT

MATERIALS

None.

PREPARATION

None.

ACTION

Mark a starting line. Divide the group into two or more teams. On the word 'go' each team forms themselves into a straight line extending from the starting-point. The first player in each team steps forward from the starting line as far as he can. The next person places a foot behind the stretched out foot of the first player and extends his other foot as far as he can reach. This procedure continues until the teams have formed a line as long as possible. The object is to make a line as far as they can in as quick a time as possible. Teams can be disqualified or penalised if anyone falls over. Award ten points to the longest team and five points for the fastest team in place.

COMMENT

A physical contact game which is fun.

ROUNDERS

MATERIALS

A beach or tennis ball, a bat or a tennis racket. Alternatively, players can use the palms of their hands to hit the ball.

PREPARATION

Mark out a course as shown in *Figure 10.4*.

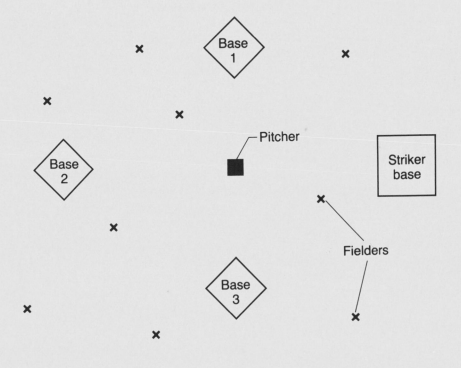

Figure 10.4

ACTION

Divide the group into two teams. Toss a coin to see who will bat first. The opposing team members spread themselves out in positions to be able to catch the ball when it is hit by the striker. The first player from the batting team stands on the striker base holding a bat. The pitcher throws the ball and the striker hits it as far as possible. He then attempts to run around the other bases and back to the striker base. If he thinks he may not make it before a fielder returns the ball to the pitcher, he may halt at one of the bases. When the next striker hits the ball, he must then run on to another base or try to make it all the way round. Not more than two players are allowed on a base. If a ball is caught by a fielder after being hit by a striker, the striker is out. If the ball has been thrown back to the pitcher and a player is between bases, that player is also out. Allow each person in the team an opportunity to bat and then have the teams change over. The team with the most complete runs at the end of the game wins.

VARIATION

Kick-a-ball   Lay out the pitch as for rounders. Instead of using a bat, the striker kicks the ball as far as possible. If the ball is returned and placed on the striker base while anyone is between two of the bases, he is out.

COMMENT

Use a tennis racket for the very energetic. Slow the game down by having the players use their hands to hit the ball and, if necessary, insist that players walk at all times. Chairs can also be placed on the bases to allow players to rest.

ALPHABETICAL LIST
OF GAMES